Managing Customer Service

Kirby LRC
Middlesbrough College
Roman Road
Middlesbrough
TS5 5PJ

Managing Customer Service

Jenny Hayes
and
Frances Dredge

Gower

Published by
Gower Publishing Limited
Gower House
Croft Road
Aldershot
Hampshire GU11 3HR
England

Gower
Old Post Road
Brookfield
Vermont 05036
USA

British Library Cataloguing in Publication Data
    Hayes, Jenny
    Managing customer service
    1. Customer services
    I. Title II. Dredge, Frances
    658.8'12

ISBN 0 566 08005 2

Typeset in Palatino by Jenny Hayes and printed in Great Britain by MPG Books Ltd, Bodmin, Cornwall

Contents

Acknowledgements

We would particularly like to thank Dr Paul Booth of Abas UK Ltd for his helpfulness in checking the technical details contained in Chapter 8 and helping to create some of the web pages that support this chapter.

The assistance of Julia Scott of Gower in checking the first draft and suggesting some useful changes was also greatly appreciated.

Naturally, any errors that remain are solely the responsibility of the authors.

JH
FD

Introduction

Customer service has a long history — from the moment the first humans figured out that it was better to barter with their neighbours than to try to do everything themselves, there have been 'customers'. For a long time, customer care was an intensely personal service. Shopkeepers, tailors, armourers and vendors of every kind knew each of their customers personally and could predict their wants and needs. There was little choice on offer and few consumers could afford luxury goods, so it was fairly easy to meet expectations.

However, the era of mass production, mass-marketing and multinational corporations has broken the link between customers and suppliers and created the need for professional customer service people. These service representatives have to tread a fine line between pleasing the customer and abiding by their organization's rules and policies.

If you have the responsibility for managing even a part of that task, then this book was written for you. It was written to be practical and down to earth. Customer service management is a very demanding role as it requires you to wear many 'hats' simultaneously. Some of the hats you may have to juggle include:

- **Business manager** — making sure that you optimize resource use to maximize profit.

- **People manager** — you have to lead your team of service staff in such a way that keeps them motivated and positive about their jobs.

- **Trainer** — you have to coach your staff in the skills of good customer service.

- **Quality manager** — you have to set standards for performance that ensure customer satisfaction.

- **Customer champion** — you have to represent the customer's viewpoint within your organization.

- **Mediator** — you have to negotiate agreement with customers that fit within your organization's objectives and policy framework.

This book addresses all of these issues, but we hope it does so in a practical, 'hands-on' way, as the last thing you probably need right now is a 'heavy read' on abstruse business topics.

How can this book help?

The book is structured as follows:

Part 1 looks at the more general management issues. Chapter 1 briefly reviews the case for investing in customer service and asks you to think about what defines good customer service in your marketplace. The next chapter takes up the theme of defining good customer service and discusses the importance of understanding your customers. It looks at a variety of ways in which you can get to grips with understanding the needs of customers with whom you don't have much personal contact. It also looks at the role that quality programmes can play in fostering good customer service practices.

Chapter 3 addresses the key management issues for customer service and these include setting standards of service, leading and motivating the customer service team, organizing an efficient system that will deliver good service and managing the relevant resources.

Part 2 of the book focuses on the practical skills required for good customer service to be delivered. Central to service is the issue of communication, and the first four chapters of Part 2 consider various aspects of communication — starting with an overview and then picking out face-to-face meetings, telephone use and letter-writing as central competencies for the customer service representative. Each topic is discussed in terms of standards, skills and exercises with a view to encouraging higher levels of performance by staff.

The information superhighway is starting to deliver real benefits for customers in a variety of marketplaces and some issues concerning the use of both email and web sites for customer services are examined in Chapter 8. This new form of telecommunication will become increasingly popular so it is worth being aware of its benefits and drawbacks which are outlined in summary form towards the end of this chapter.

Chapters 9 and 10 consider the vexed question of unhappy customers. These will only ever be a minority of cases, but it is vital to deal with them successfully. Chapter 9 tackles the issue of handling customer complaints in a way that should lead to greater satisfaction and increased customer loyalty. Chapter 10 looks at what to do when things have gone badly wrong and customers are furious about the way they have been dealt with.

Chapter 11 looks at the potential for using customer service staff to increase sales volume by being more pro-active in their dealings with customers. Instead of passively answering questions, staff can be encouraged to do a little probing of their own and suggest solutions to potential customers.

The final chapter briefly discusses the need to promote customer care as a mission for the whole organization and looks at ways of encouraging all staff to recognize their responsibilities as links in the customer service chain.

Part 1
General management issues

1
The significance of customer service

Why is customer service so important today?

Customer service has always been important, but today's customers have so much more freedom of choice than in previous decades that the marketplace for every product or service is considerably more competitive. In days gone by, people would shop at their local grocery store, but nowadays people can choose whether to visit a local high street or one of a number of out-of-town superstores. This choice doesn't just extend to consumer goods either, businesses can now pick up the phone and order goods from anywhere in the world.

Service is not the only issue that decides where people make their purchases, but it is a very important one. In many surveys of both consumer and business purchasing, service often ranks higher than price in people's priorities. Service can give a company 'competitive edge' and can offset other factors.

> One of the chief purchasers for Sainsbury's admitted that Marks & Spencer had an advantage over his own chain. He told an interviewer that because of the store's reputation for quality, people perceived shortages in supply differently than they would for his own store. If Sainsbury's runs out of milk, he said, you can hear the customers complaining about how inefficient the store is — they get angry with Sainsbury's. But if Marks & Spencer runs out of milk, you hear the customers saying 'I should have got up earlier' — in other words, they blame themselves rather than the shop.
>
> This difference in customer attitude can be critical in retaining market share and achieving greater profitability. In this example, it allows Marks & Spencer to charge premium prices for its products, whereas Sainsbury's has to compete with other stores to try to offer best value.

Customer service is definitely a key issue for business suppliers where customer–supplier relationships can last for many years and involve significant amounts of money. A business purchaser may not move an account for a small price saving if he or she knows that good service is guaranteed by an existing supplier. Issues like reliability, warranties, punctuality, flexibility of delivery, personal rapport and ease of ordering can all make significant impact on the buyer's sense of 'value for money'.

Why is it important to retain customers by offering good service?

There is a clear business justification for building customer loyalty. It is usually far cheaper to retain existing customers than it is to find new ones, which can be both a difficult and expensive process. Existing customers are already known to the organization and can be contacted easily. A loyal customer may spend many thousands of pounds with an organization over the years. Especially if he or she is encouraged to do so by the careful management of the account and scrupulous attention to delivering the product or service as promised. It is therefore easier and more profitable to deal with existing customers than to have to search out new ones each time a company needs to make a sale.

> Consider the example set by car manufacturers. These companies spend hundreds of thousands of pounds promoting their cars through TV adverts, mailings, discount offers etc. If a person only buys a car off the manufacturer once then the company has gained maybe £10,000. But if that customer returns to the dealer to have the car serviced and repaired every year for three years (the average time a new car purchaser keeps a model), then he or she may have spent a further £2,000. And, if pleased by the service offered by the dealer, the customer trades in the old car for a newer model, then the manufacturer has gained another £10,000. Multiply these figures out over the lifetime of an average car buyer and you begin to see how the numbers rapidly add up. Customer loyalty can add up to a very healthy profit margin.

It is well-known that existing customers are more likely to buy from a company than from 'strangers'. If their accounts have been handled correctly, existing customers:

- already know what's available
- have faith in the company supplying the correct items on time
- understand the terms of purchase
- feel confident that they will get exactly what they expect
- feel reassured that the company is reliable

actors make it easier to buy from a known
r than from a new company. They also explain
s so hard to tempt other companies' customers
ıt a new supplier. But this is only true if the
customer is satisfied by the service that he or she has
received.

However, if a customer has experienced bad
service from a company, the chances are that the
company will never know about it. Surveys have
shown that on average only 5 per cent of unhappy
customers actually complain to the offending
organization. The other 95 per cent stop buying and
tell their friends, neighbours and colleagues never to
do business with that company.

This does not mean that you should despair if a
customer's order goes wrong. There is a very positive
side to handling these problems. If you can deal with
a customer complaint quickly, efficiently and to the
customer's satisfaction , you will have created a
customer who is *more* loyal to your organization than
one who has never had any problems.

From the point of view of customer service
management, problems really are opportunities to
keep hold of business for years to come.

What is excellent customer service?

Customer service can be defined as the way in which
an organization handles the interactions between
itself (in the person of its staff) and its customers.
These interactions can be many and varied and they
can last over several years or for just a few moments.
However, each of these transactions between the
individual customer and the individual employee
needs attention and appropriate handling. The role of
the customer service manager is to ensure that staff

endeavour at all times to *satisfy the expectations of the customers.*

There are many ingredients in the customer service recipe and some specific issues are tackled later in this book. But for an overview of what your customers consider important, you will need to stop reading for a moment and try to put yourself in their shoes. What would you want from your organization if you were its customer?

You might want to think about the following general points:

- **Timeliness** — how quickly can you respond to customer demands?
- **Flexibility** — do you give your customers precisely what they want or are they constrained to buy what you can supply?
- **Friendliness** — do members of your team work hard to create a friendly environment in which customers feel welcomed by your organization?
- **Honesty** — do you deal fairly with your customers, telling them upfront what you can and what you cannot do for them?
- **Expectations** — do you keep your promises (not just the ones your staff make personally, but also the ones that you advertise in your sales literature)?
- **Quality** — do you get it right first time, every time? Do you have clear and measurable targets for the quality of your goods and services?
- **Problems** — what do you do when things go wrong?
- **Value** — what do you do to build value into the products or services that you deliver?

- **Reliability** — can customers trust you and your products/services?

- **Communication** — do you actively listen to your customers and act on their comments and suggestions?

These are just some of the elements that combine to produce customer satisfaction when done well. They are discussed in more detail in specific chapters later in this book — as is the issue of discovering what your customers really value about the service that you offer.

2
Defining 'good service'

'Good service' needs to be driven by customers' needs and expectations. If your service fails to satisfy your customers then no matter how fantastic it may appear to you, it is *not* good service. Unfortunately, this doesn't mean that you can just ask your customers what they want and then give it to them. This approach won't give you the *whole* story — many customers don't know what they really want until someone offers it to them.

In a different context Professor Charles Handy calls this the 'Aha' effect where you recognize that an idea, product or service is what you really wanted, but never realized until someone demonstrated it to you. You want your customers to say: 'Aha, that's just what I wanted, but I could never describe it until now.'

If you can tap into that recognition of an unfulfilled need, you can create a strong and lasting bond with your customers. It is certainly a way to get ahead of the competition and ensure a deep-seated level of customer satisfaction.

Personal computers

A good example of the fact that people don't know
that they need a product until it's given to them is the
invention of the personal computer — in particular
the Apple Macintosh. Up to the early 1970s,
computers had been large pieces of equipment owned
by companies and used by highly skilled technical
staff. It took a visionary outlook to think about
putting the power of one of these machines on to the
desk of an individual — and more importantly, to
make it instantly usable.

The Apple story

Technological developments made the personal computer
possible, but it took the imagination and creative flair of
Steve Jobs and Steve Wozniak, the founders of Apple, to
make the personal computer usable by the ordinary person
without lots of special training. Jobs and Wozniak built the
first Macintosh and started to sell it without conducting any
market surveys or asking customers what they wanted —
they did it on 'gut instinct' and invented a runaway bestseller. In the early days of Apple, it couldn't make its
personal computers fast enough to meet demand and this
was because it was the first company to make a 'friendly'
and easy-to-use computer.

Customers didn't know they wanted Macintosh
computers until they saw them, and then suddenly, they
knew they wanted them.

However, the spectacular early success of Apple has been
matched by its recent decline — in part because it has failed
to listen to its customers. There are many reasons for
Apple's poor performance, but closer attention to the needs
and expectations of its customers might have made for a
different ending to this story.

The 'Aha' factor requires a leap of imagination, but it
does not usually replace the need for a detailed
understanding of your customers' requirements. This
understanding is absolutely vital if you are to be able
to match the features of the product or service you are

offering to the needs of the customer. Customers who
feel misunderstood, ignored or dissatisfied do not
return.

Understanding the customer

Understanding the customer requires effort on a
variety of levels and involves a number of different
functions in an organization. However, the people
with responsibility for talking to the customer and
organizing any service that is provided (from
technical help to ordering, billing and handling
queries) must be able to 'talk the customers'
language'. Managers with responsibility for customer
service cannot afford to dismiss sector or trend
knowledge as being purely the province of the
marketing department. Even if much 'broad brush'
customer information is gathered by the marketing
department or by market researchers, the customer
service manager must understand how and why this
data is gathered (so its real worth can be evaluated)
and be able to compare it with the information
gathered by customer service operatives (including
anecdotal information — customer 'stories' can be
very revealing if examined in the right light).

Gathering information

Companies can use a variety of approaches to gather
information — both quantitative and qualitative —
about their customers and potential customers
including:

- **Market surveys** — conducted by market
  researchers to investigate specific aspects of a

market or of a market's perceptions of a range of products/services. These tend to result in quantitative information of the form: 'X per cent of the respondents said that they strongly preferred dealing with companies over the telephone rather than going into a branch,' or 'X per cent of respondents said they have a personal computer that runs Windows95'. These statistical measures have to be interpreted carefully, remembering that it is not always possible for surveyors to select people at random and therefore the sample might be biased, and that the answers given will depend on the questions asked. Leading questions will get more answers of a particular kind than balanced questions on the same topic. Survey design is a specialized professional activity and when done badly can negate the value of the survey. If your organization does conduct surveys of this nature and you find the results surprising or not in keeping with your daily experiences of customer preferences, ask to see the questions that were asked.

- **Industry/market trends** — these paint a possible picture of the future, based on an understanding of the current situation. For example, in the computer industry there is a clear trend for the processing power of PCs to increase while prices decrease. Trends are also important because they help to form customers' expectations — a person looking to purchase a PC today will not feel the buying decision is urgent because prices might rise unless he or she is contemplating the purchase of an older model that is being phased out.

- **Focus panels** — getting actual customers into groups and asking them to discuss what their expectations and perceptions of a company's goods/services are and how they might be improved. This qualitative feedback is usually very specific and detailed, but may lack an appreciation of the broader picture. It is also anchored to the present as customers are likely to think about what they currently get rather than visualize future potential. Focus groups also tend to be self-selecting in that anyone willing to serve on such a panel is probably a 'loyal' customer already. This can lead to a disparity between focus group views and those of the average customer.

- **Surveys of non-customers** — it can be very helpful to specifically question people or businesses who considered your company's goods/services but rejected them in favour of your competitors'. This can give you considerable insight into your company's perceived strengths and weaknesses as compared to the competition. The problem with only asking existing customers is that you get a biased viewpoint — talking to non-customers can supply the other point of view.

- **Customer surveys** — these can be done through the use of 'feedback' forms, telephone surveys, mailed questionnaires or the careful recording of reports from customer service staff. The aim is to build up a picture of what your customers are saying and thinking about your organization and its goods/services. Even relatively satisfied customers may be experiencing some 'niggles' with your service, so it's important to listen to them as carefully as you can. If minor problems can be addressed before they have become raging irritants then you go a long way to ensure customer loyalty.

The above sources are all specific to your company (apart from possibly the market trend information), however, you can also 'buy' customer information in the form of published surveys and reports. There are companies which specialize in providing a range of types of market information in a variety of forms. It is also worth reading the industry press for your market or industry sector as these publications should contain a wide range of market-relevant information. They will also help you and your staff to keep in touch with industry developments and make communicating with customers more effective.

Listen to your staff

Staff should be encouraged to pass on customer viewpoints. It is important not to blame the messenger for the message. It can be hard to listen to critical comments relayed by staff, especially if you think the customer has got a faulty impression, but if you don't learn to listen without interrupting and without getting defensive or critical of the staff member, then this source of feedback will dry up.

If a staff member relays a customer service story which suggests that they didn't handle the customer very well, then it's more helpful to explore the different ways they could have handled the situation better. This will have a more positive effect on their future behaviour than simply shouting at them or cutting them off in mid-story.

Your aim is to coach your staff to do better next time — to learn from their experience. If you do this in an unpleasant fashion, then the next time they handle something badly, they will try to keep that fact hidden from you, and they may never improve their performance as a result. It is also important not to jump to conclusions — try to listen to the whole story before you make any response.

What are your competitors offering your customers?

You are unlikely to be alone in your marketplace and one of the factors that helps to define customer expectations is the activity of your competitors. For example, your customers may be very happy with a delivery lead-time of a week — until they discover that one of your competitors offers guaranteed next-day delivery. It is not enough to emulate your competitors, but nor can you afford to be left behind. When Tesco first introduced its customer loyalty card — offering rewards to regular customers — Sainsbury's openly scoffed at the idea. However, when Tesco outperformed Sainsbury's and took the coveted number one supermarket spot, Sainsbury's rapidly introduced its own loyalty card scheme.

Sometimes, being second on to the market with a service can be a good thing as it gives you a chance to learn from the frontrunner's mistakes. But being last on to the market with any kind of product or service usually means that you are going to have an uphill battle to win new customers over — unless you can offer them a significant advantage if they buy from you.

It is worth keeping a 'watching brief' on the activities of your competitors, because you will need the information either to change your own activities or to devise a good explanation as to why your competitor's approach is not as attractive as your own. If you don't know what your competitors are offering — especially in terms of customer service — you can be caught flatfooted by your customers querying why *you* don't offer the same type of service.

It also means that you can take advantage of the customer research that your competitor carries out — if it introduces a service because its customers have told it they want this service, then maybe you should be introducing such a service too, or at least talking to your customers about it.

Your customers are likely to be the subjects of your competitors' marketing campaigns and special offers, so it's vital to stay a step ahead of their game.

What do all customers want?

While it's unhelpful to make sweeping assumptions, there are some general expectations that most customers have:

- *Efficiency* — customers expect that customer service operatives know what they are doing and are applying the organization's policies correctly. Customers do not expect to be kept waiting needlessly.

- *Honesty* — customers expect to be dealt with professionally and honestly. They do not expect to be lied to.

- *Politeness* — customers expect to be dealt with politely, even if they are making a complaint. They do not expect to hear abusive language, to be patronized or to be dismissed curtly.

- *Respect* — customers expect to be treated in a way that recognizes their value as human beings, even if they are not paying customers but the recipients of some service. Disrespect can encourage aggression or a refusal to deal with the organization.

- *Follow-through* — customers expect to be able to rely on the organization doing what the member of staff has said that it will do. If a service representative makes a promise, it must be kept.

Quality programmes and their links to customer care

Total quality management (TQM) has been heavily hyped in the past few years with thousands of companies applying to be assessed to the ISO 9000 quality standard. How does this affect customer service?

One of the fundamental tenets of TQM is that the assurance of customer satisfaction is the keystone of success. If a company does not achieve customer satisfaction then all its other activities are pointless. However, TQM defines customer satisfaction in a broad way as it introduces the idea of 'internal customers'. This concept has been defined to make the goal of customer satisfaction relevant to everyone in an organization, not just the front-line staff who actually deal with the 'real' customers.

An internal customer is anyone in the organization who receives your work, so a PA might view his or her boss as his or her internal customer because he or she supplies this 'customer' with work. Managers can view their staff as 'customers' because they supply them with instructions, work and targets. The aim of this approach is to 'personalize' the abstract requirement to satisfy the end customer by defining this goal in terms that are immediately relevant to every single employee. It creates a 'quality chain' of customer/supplier relationships that runs through the whole organization and clarifies the responsibilities of each individual with regard to the overriding objective of customer satisfaction.

This should help the people who actually deal with the external customers by ensuring that they get the service they need from their internal colleagues to meet those customers' needs. Suddenly, the customer is not on the outside looking in, but is *within* the organization, driving forward improvements in all work processes.

In this way, customer satisfaction becomes a realistic and achievable goal for every member of staff.

What is quality?

Quality is technically defined as 'fitness for purpose' or 'conformance to specifications' — and this is distinctly different from the general use of the word to mean 'excellence'. For this reason a ballpoint pen is just as much a quality product as a gold-plated fountain pen or a Pentium-based personal computer — if the specification is that the product is to be used for writing. Cost is an element of quality — there is such a thing as being over-specified and therefore over-priced: if you want to write a note for the milk-deliverer changing your order to two pints a day, you don't need a word processor you need a ballpoint pen and a scrap of paper.

Quality service means providing the right level of service to meet customer needs. And this is why it is so important to discover what those needs are, so that your whole service operation can be driven by them. Customer service is a major professional challenge because customer needs are frequently multi-variable, often inconsistent with each other and they do change over time. You are trying to hit a target that changes shape, colour and races about. It's not impossible, but it does call for skill, accuracy, flexibility, determination and the ability to anticipate future demands.

However, you can only perform this exacting job if the rest of the organization supports your efforts. This means that you have to communicate customer requirements further down the line. If your staff are 'let down' by product flaws, billing errors, slow repairs or any other internal factor, then it's your responsibility to raise the problem at managerial levels and get it fixed. The long-term health of the organization rests on its managers being prepared to upset applecarts in the pursuit of customer satisfaction.

Employee involvement

Another fundamental tenet of TQM is the involvement and participation of all employees. Everyone can make a contribution to the overall objective of customer satisfaction.

There are several mechanisms for this participation that can encourage its effectiveness:

- **Quality circles** — groups of employees who have volunteered to look at ways of improving the work in their particular area. These are called 'circles' by some and 'quality action teams' or 'continual improvement teams' by others. The aim is to subject work processes to detailed evaluation and improvement by the people who actually perform those processes.

- **Empowerment** — this is a rather clumsy term coined to express the delegation of authority downwards, or the release of enterprise and initiative at grassroots level, depending on your point of view. The aim is to ensure that decisions are made by those closest to the situation whenever possible (and within the usual organizational constraints). So if a customer approaches one of your staff complaining about late delivery, it might be appropriate for your staff member (no matter how junior) to be able to authorize a 10 per cent discount on the next order as part of the apology to the customer for the failure to deliver, rather than having to ask you to deal with the matter. Empowerment only works if it is totally supported by senior management — if they don't stand behind the decisions made by junior staff then the employees soon get the message that it's empowerment in name but not in action.

- **Continuous improvement programmes** — quality is partly about challenging the *status quo* and looking for potential improvements in service or product quality all the time, regardless of whether anyone has complained lately. It is pro-active rather than reactive and aims to prevent problems arising rather than fix them as they happen. One of the paradoxes of customer satisfaction is that as quickly as you delight the customer by exceeding their expectations, they raise those expectations. As people benefit from higher standards of service, so they begin to expect them and what might once have been considered as 'outstanding' quickly becomes the norm. This is why you have to make it a priority for all staff to constantly seek out new and better ways of serving your customers.

- **Suggestion schemes** — the drive for continual improvement calls for the active participation of all employees, and suggestion schemes are a formal method of encouraging and capturing the

bright ideas of all employees. These schemes can
be incredibly effective — Land Rover found that
by strongly encouraging suggestions from its staff,
it increased from one suggestion per ten
employees in 1988 to three suggestions per
employee in 1992. The company has estimated that
employee suggestions have saved it on the order
of £1.5 million. An effective suggestion scheme is
well publicized throughout the organization, any
suggestions are reviewed speedily and a reply
guaranteed in a short space of time and good ideas
are recognized and implemented with some
element of reward going to the inventor.
Suggestion schemes that are slow, give little or no
feedback as to why suggestions are rejected and
which offer no recognition or reward to people
who have good ideas tend to fail.

Each of these mechanisms for encouraging active
participation on the part of all employees calls for a
'partnership' approach on the part of the management
team. If managers feel threatened by ideas from those
lower down the hierarchy or continue to operate in
authoritarian ways despite paying lip service to
quality ideals, then these initiatives will not succeed.
Surveys of the effectiveness of TQM approaches have
repeatedly shown that one of the key determining
factors in their success is the commitment of the
management team.

It is not enough to talk about quality and to launch
TQM initiatives designed to enlist the participation of
employees — you have to 'live' the quality culture
and embrace a 'teamwork' approach to decision-
making and problem-solving.

Summary

The key points discussed by this chapter revolve around the definition of good service as being the *satisfaction of customer expectations*. This in turn, means that it is important to understand customers — both in terms of who they are and what they expect:

- at a very broad level, this means understanding your marketplace,

- at a more specific level, this means building profiles of 'typical' customers,

- at the detailed level this means keeping good records on individual customers and finding out as much about them as possible and using this information to anticipate their needs.

There are several mechanisms you can use to support your understanding of your customers and these include market surveys, focus groups, feedback forms and surveys of non-customers.

Customer service is an integral part of total quality management, so the adoption of TQM principles can really improve the status of customer service in an organization. As satisfying the needs of the customer become a 'core' mission for the organization, so it should become easier to provide the level of service that your customers really appreciate. However, TQM calls for the active participation of all employees and this means that managers have to be prepared to adopt a more flexible and teamwork-oriented outlook than has traditionally been the case. If managers resist the delegation of authority and decision-making to more 'junior' employees, then any TQM initiative will be sabotaged.

3

Key management issues for customer service

People management skills are vital if you lead a customer service team because no matter how high-tech the industry, service is delivered by people. Motivated, enthusiastic and well-trained staff will deliver top-level service, while well-equipped, but negative or resentful staff will deliver inadequate service. People management is a wide and challenging subject area and this chapter cannot hope to cover all the issues. So the aim of this chapter is to pick out some of the most relevant issues for the customer service manager and suggest follow-up reading for some other important issues.

Motivation is the key to positive staff attitudes. It cannot be applied piecemeal. The idea that you can get people to feel committed to their work simply by offering them bonuses for certain levels of performance is over-simplistic. Staff are motivated when they feel involved — when they feel that they can make a difference and that their efforts are recognized by others.

Practical ways of motivating people form the first part of this chapter. We look at how you can use non-financial incentives to encourage staff to adopt a positive approach to customer service. Some motivational principles are outlined and their practical implications are discussed.

We have also included a short section on the particular needs of part-time staff in this respect, as 'flexible working' is becoming more and more important especially in customer service roles.

In addition, the third part of this chapter looks at some issues of resource and system management. Even motivated and highly enthusiastic staff need the right tools for the job and deserve to have their efforts supported by an efficient system. It can be very demoralizing to have one's best efforts constantly undermined by an inadequate organization.

The vital issue of standards is tackled in the fourth and final part of this chapter. Clear objectives and well-defined guidelines make it possible for you to give staff more freedom in the way they handle aspects of their work while still promoting consistent and excellent levels of service across the board. In some ways this is what 'empowerment' is all about — delegating decisions to the person nearest to the 'problem' or opportunity and providing a clear framework to guide the decision-making process. This allows people to use their own judgement while working within the policies of their organization.

1 Motivation

Staff morale is an important element in guaranteeing good customer service. Gloomy, dispirited or resentful staff will not optimize customer contacts and they may even encourage customers to go elsewhere. Ensuring that staff are motivated is not necessarily an easy managerial task, but it is an essential one.

The problem facing the manager of customer service staff can sometimes be made more difficult by the generally low status of such staff. Even though lip service is paid to the search for service excellence, the staff who deliver it at the sharp edge are often regarded as relatively unimportant. This can have two unfortunate results: staff aren't allowed to show initiative (because it is presumed they don't have any) and investment in training of such staff is regarded as low priority.

This attitude does not encourage a positive response from the staff concerned — they may feel undervalued, under-resourced and unrewarded. As a manager, you can't 'pour' motivation into your service team — motivation is an internal drive. But you can help to create the conditions in which motivation thrives.

The principles underlying motivation

Psychologists have studied what motivates people for many years and have developed many theories to explain why people do the things they do. Many of these theories are of little practical use for managers. However, one theory of motivation which has stood the test of time and has proved useful to managers is that proposed by Abraham Maslow. He defined a 'hierarchy of needs' and regarded people as trying to fulfil those needs in hierarchical order. His hierarchy is shown in the box below and he suggested that people would want to fulfil their basic physiological needs (the base of the hierarchy) before moving on to tackle their social needs for example. This implies that as they fulfil each set of needs people's underlying motivation changes as they focus on new needs.

Need	Definition	Work-related requirements
Self-actualisation	Fulfilling one's potential by developing and exercising talents and abilities	Being given the chance to stretch oneself by being given new responsibilities and challenges
Esteem	Being shown recognition by others — praise, status etc. bolstering one's esteem in the eyes of others (and oneself)	Promotion, praise, awards for the quality of work
Social	Feeling a sense of belonging and being involved in social interaction	Being a member of a team, participating in social activities connected to work
Safety and security	Feeling and being safe both physically and mentally	Job security, pensions as well as safe conditions of work
Physiological	Basic needs such as food, water and shelter	A salary that pays enough to live on, acceptable working conditions

Another psychologist, Herzberg, added to this understanding of motivation by suggesting that there are two types of factors that influence people's level of motivation:

- Hygiene factors like pay and job security

- Motivational factors like job satisfaction, autonomy and fulfilment

Herzberg's main point was that the things that create motivation in a person are often not the tangibles like pay — which is taken as 'deserved' — but the intangibles like encouragement, recognition and status. However, these have to be fundamental parts of the corporate culture. They can't be tacked on as afterthoughts. There is no point in telling people that they are wonderful if you actually treat them like small children who have to be supervised every minute of the day. It is essential that the organization lives its motivational ideals and does not just talk about them.

Practical tips

Encouragement

Encouragement is probably one of the most under-rated tools a manager has at his or her disposal. The positive reinforcement of employees' sense of self-worth by praise and reassurance can have a very strong effect on employees' inner self-motivation.

Make the job feel worthwhile

It is hard to be motivated to do a job that you feel is fundamentally trivial or worthless and that's why it is so important to build up the value of a customer service job in employees' eyes. If a negative or derogatory view of the customer representative's role is purveyed from the top, this can totally undermine staff. It tends also to lead to the sort of training that suggests that simply wearing a false smile for every customer and using their name repeatedly will build up rapport — nothing could be further from the truth.

In reality dealing with customers is a serious professional challenge — even in situations where customer contact is fleeting (as in the retail environment) or over the telephone. The customer service representative is required to create a sense of 'welcome' and 'good service' by using their personal social skills as well as their job skills. He or she is the 'face' of the organization and his or her attitude towards the job and, by implication the customer, is a vital part of the equation in creating customer retention.

For people to believe that the job they do is valuable:

- It has to be set in context — what's the big picture?
- It has to be reinforced by the managers of the company — no undermining comments along the line of 'they're only customer service operatives, what would they know?'
- Staff have to be given some opportunity to influence the way that they do their jobs. Yes, consistency and procedure is important, but this doesn't mean that staff shouldn't be encouraged to suggest ideas for improvement. After all, who has the most contact with customers — your staff or the marketing team at head office?
- There is a difference between service and servility — although your company policy should be to champion its customers, this does not mean that customers are always right. Your staff need to be trained to defuse difficult situations, but they shouldn't feel obliged to endure abusive or threatening behaviour. Your staff will feel more confident and motivated if they are secure in the knowledge that you will support them in their actions and decisions in tricky situations.

Team spirit

There has been a lot of discussion about the value of teamwork in the workplace and some researchers are not convinced that putting people into teams translates into increased productivity. However, teamwork can offer advantages in terms of flexibility and increased motivation.

There are always a few lone wolves, but there is no doubt that people want to belong to a group. This 'social need' has been identified by psychologists as a basic human drive. It is possible to use this 'need to belong' to build teams that motivate themselves. Team members set expectations and standards for each other with peer pressure as a powerful force acting to encourage people to meet these expectations.

There are pitfalls in creating teams: one of which is that it is possible to create a 'them and us' atmosphere which can be unfortunate if it fosters aggressive competition between teams, but disastrous if it is the customers who are seen as 'them' and the service team as 'us'. It is vital that 'service' is the cornerstone of any team's objectives. To prevent a sense of the 'customer as interruption or even opponent' from creeping in, a clear focus needs to be placed on the customer as the key to success for the team and the individual.

Team members can be motivated in three ways:

- **Task** — a team needs to have clear objectives (these are essential if the team is to work smoothly in any case).
- **Group** — the interaction between team members is important in motivational terms. If people like and respect one another, they are more likely to encourage each other to do a good job and to help one another to achieve.

- **Individual** — team members still need to be treated as individuals with their own needs and drives.

Team briefings can be great opportunities to deliver a motivating message. It's important that you bring out the positive side of any message that you have to communicate at these briefings. This doesn't mean smiling while you deliver bad news, that would clearly be inappropriate and foster distrust. But it does mean explaining the positive reasons for changes in policy and procedure. In particular it means resisting the temptation to pass on any negative feelings you may have about a senior management decision. If you undermine senior management, you undermine your own authority and undercut any sense that your staff might have that they are working for a worthwhile organization.

Money can't buy you motivation...

Money alone is not a sufficient motivator — it helps and it can direct behavioural activity down certain routes (witness the way that sales staff are paid commission to encourage them to close sales), but of itself it won't create a motivational atmosphere. In particular, the problem with a one-factor solution (offer a financial incentive for a certain activity) is that you get a one-step solution and that might not be what is required. Suppose that you offer customer service staff a bonus for each sale that they close. This action may boost sales levels in the short term, but in the long term you may damage customer retention rates because service staff may become less interested in giving good service than they are in getting another order, and this may make them less helpful, seem hurried or even 'pushy' to the customer.

Customer retention is a far more powerful key to business success than a short-term climb in sales. By only rewarding one activity (closing a sale) you send a very distorted message about your company's values to your frontline service employees. You can talk up the service ethos until you are 'blue in the face', but your powerful underlying message is that only sales count.

2 Managing part-timers — a special case?

One of the many challenges of managing customer service staff is the widespread and growing use of part-time employees. These workers give organizations the flexibility to cope with peaks and troughs of customer demand while keeping costs low. However, it can be difficult to integrate them into a mainly full-time team because there can be a tendency to treat them as 'second class citizens'. This is a grave mistake as part-timers can contribute as much as full-time staff if they are encouraged to be full members of the team. The only thing that part-timers give less of is their time — they can put as much if not more energy, enthusiasm and expertise into their work, aided by the fact that they have less time in which to become bored or cynical.

There can be drawbacks to employing part-time workers. Part-timers may have competing commitments (for example, students working to support their studies, mothers working shorter hours while caring for younger children) and they may be less loyal. But loyalty is a 'chicken and egg' type issue. Are part-timers less loyal to their employers simply because they know that they are often paid less than their full-time colleagues, are more likely to lose their jobs if redundancies are made and have to work for managers who regard them as 'second best'?

If you want to get the best from your part-time staff, your first priority is to make them feel part of the team and not outsiders. It is very important to communicate relevant information to them and include them in any team discussions. It's also essential that work is allocated fairly and part-timers don't get dumped with 'dogsbody work' because they are less likely to complain.

Research by the Roffey Park Management Institute has shown that part-time staff consider the following factors to be important to them in their work:

- They want to feel challenged by their work and given opportunities to learn new skills, whether as a result of job rotation or by being given extra responsibilities.

- They want to feel that they have the support of their manager and are not considered to be second-best employees.

- They want to be trusted with their work.

- They want to feel valued and appreciated by their manager and colleagues — a simple 'thank you' or credit for a job well done may be all that it takes.

- They want opportunities to make suggestions and see them acted on.

- They want to be invited to join in any work 'social' events — to be treated as full members of the team.

These factors are important to any member of a work team, but part-timers often feel marginalized by their status, so the manager that takes a bit more care over

these employees may be rewarded by greater
commitment and a more flexible approach to work.

3   Effective systems

Efficiency and effectiveness are not the same. You can
have efficient systems that do not deliver the required
results. The most important job you can do as a
resource manager is to examine what the results of
your team's work should be. An effective system is
one that delivers those results every time.

However, it is important to devise efficient
processes to produce the desired results. You may
have trained your staff to be charming, courteous and
pro-active, but they also need to be able to find
information quickly and be able to respond efficiently
to requests. This calls for careful organization and
work planning.
If your organization has been in existence for some
time, it may have developed several processes and
activities that now require review. No system lasts
forever and processes which were effective when put
in place five years ago may have become distorted by
the passage of time or outdated by changes in
technology or organizational objectives.

If your aim is to ensure consistent and effective
service that will satisfy your customers, then
everything you and your staff do has to be evaluated
in the light of that overriding objective. Do you find
that you or your staff are having to work 'around'
inconvenient or awkward work processes? If so, it's
time to look for new methods.

Quality management programmes emphasize the
need for continuous improvement, so encourage all
your staff to be on the look out for new ways of
performing activities that will help them to work

more efficiently or help your customers to get a better level of service.

Resource management

What resources do you need to ensure that your customers are satisfied? These include people, equipment, materials and money. An understaffed customer service department is likely to disappoint some customers who are made to wait or not given a sufficiently personal service. You need the tools for the job, even something as simple as more telephone lines can make a big difference to your effectiveness. Too few lines or an inefficient switchboard system can drive customers mad if they have to wait long periods for a reply or frequently get a 'busy line' signal.

One luxury hotel chain in London gives every member of staff (including cleaners, chambermaids and receptionists) a budget of £2000 per year to spend on 'customer satisfaction'. This means that if a customer complains about a problem, the staff member who hears the complaint can instantly authorize some action to resolve the situation. For example, he or she might organize for the customer to receive a pair of theatre tickets as an apology for a noisy room. The hotel chain regards such gifts as money well spent because it ensures a very high level of customer loyalty — guests keep coming back.

Managers have to cost-justify expenditure on their departments and it is up to them to produce the results which show senior managers that the money is well spent. This may mean collecting more feedback from customers than is strictly financially necessary, but as the previous chapter illustrated, you can only satisfy customer expectations if you know what these are. The more you know about your customers and their reactions to your services, the more able you are to improve their opinions of your organization.

This is why it is important to look at resource management issues from the customer's viewpoint rather than solely from an internal or organizational stance. You have a special responsibility to champion the needs of your customers as well as the usual responsibilities of ensuring that you deliver business results, keep costs low and margins high.

It is therefore appropriate to evaluate the kind of service that you offer to customers in terms of meeting their service needs, not just their product requirements. A bank account held by the telephone banking company, First Direct, offers pretty much the same terms and facilities as an account at any of the high street banks. But the company differentiates itself by offering 24-hour telephone service to all its customers. The competitive edge is in the service element of the banking package. The high street banks might argue that the friendliness and helpfulness of their local branches give them an edge, but the point is that different customers value different elements of service differently.

Looking at the service package in this light means evaluating aspects such as how to eliminate service bottlenecks (for example, using a voice mail system to offer customers the chance of leaving their name and number to be called back if they called when all the telephone operatives were engaged), speed of fulfilment (for example, the use of overnight couriers for mail-order goods), speed of response to any enquiry (for example, same-day replies to letters). This may help you to highlight any resource considerations that prevent your staff from giving the service that your customers want.

There is a saying, 'penny-wise and pound-foolish', which is particularly apposite to customer service.

Given the high costs of finding new customers, if an existing customer defects to the competition it can be cost-justified to invest in appropriate resources to boost service levels.

To be able to cost-justify this kind of expenditure on additional resources, you must measure customer retention rates (in terms of lifetime, lifelong values, re-order rates etc.) plus anecdotal evidence of referrals, as well as measuring the cost of providing the elements of the service package. You need firm evidence to convince other managers that resources devoted to customer care reap rewards through orders from contented, loyal customers.

4 Standards

It is absolutely vital that all the members of a customer service team are 'singing from the same hymn sheet'. It is confusing and irritating for customers to get different messages or levels of service depending on whom they talk to.

The setting of standards for service, efficiency and outcome are all management responsibilities. The manager defines the boundaries within which staff must work to achieve the targets which also have to be clearly defined by the manager in line with overall organizational objectives. For targets and standards to be clearly defined, they must fulfil the SMART criteria as follows:

- **Specific** — targets and standards need to be defined at a detailed level as generalized 'hand waving' just won't do. For example, stating that 'We need to give excellent service' is too vague to be useful. It's important to state specific activities or outcomes that constitute excellent service: 'Our aim is to resolve all a customer's queries in a single call.'

- **Measurable** — if it can't be measured how can anyone be sure they are reaching a standard? For example, responding to all customers' written enquiries within 48 hours is a standard of service that can be measured objectively.

Team task

Try getting together as a team to set standards. This has three major benefits:

- It helps to build a stronger team.

- It increases commitment to achieving the standards defined in this way.

- It increases understanding both of the exact detail of any standards and of the need for them.

Involving members of staff who have regular contact with customers means that any standards defined in this way are more likely to meet the customers' real requirements.

About a week before the meeting, ask everyone to prepare a list of the standards they think would be of most benefit to the customers — this will encourage them to think about the issue carefully.

In the team meeting, ask people to read out their lists and merge all the ideas together to produce a list of possible standards. Rank these ideas in order of importance and then discuss each idea with a view to evaluating its desirability. Also decide whether it can be implemented easily and immediately or whether it will require substantial changes in working processes.

Get the team to identify a subgroup of standards you can implement straightaway and agree a plan of action. Discuss how you are going to implement more 'difficult' standards and formulate a longer term plan of action for these.

Clearly these activities can be split over a number of shorter meetings rather than all carried out in a single session. But it's important to hold the meetings close together as otherwise you will lose momentum and spend too much time reminding each other of what was said last time. It is better to try to give this sort of task a sense of urgency by setting short deadlines.

- **Achievable** — it's pointless setting unrealistic standards as this will only set your staff up to fail which is demoralizing and futile. This doesn't mean that standards should be set so low that they can be easily reached, but you want to avoid setting impossible ones. The aim is to challenge your staff to stretch their skill development and offer the customer the best possible service within the framework of resource constraints (the real world).

- **Relevant** — standards must be seen to be relevant to the job in hand. This may mean explaining why you have set certain standards and what you are trying to achieve. In other words, don't hand out standards as though they were carved on tablets of stone, discuss them with staff and if possible get them involved in setting their own standards.

- **Timely** — where appropriate set time limits on actions. Set deadlines for the achievement of standards when they cannot be achieved immediately. It is important to create a sense of urgency about meeting standards of performance, otherwise they may get lost in the day-to-day bustle of activity.

Further reading

There are many management texts available in the bookshops, so we have selected just a few of the more accessible titles for your consideration:

Starting to Manage: the essential skills by Gerald Blair (Chartwell Bratt) is an enjoyable and practical book aimed at first-time managers. It is amusing and written in an anecdotal but informative way and covers many of the fundamental management skills.

The Equal Opportunities Guide by Phil Clements and Tony Spinks (Kogan Page) offers some useful insights into the problems that can arise when you have to manage a variety of different 'types' of employee. It discusses many uncomfortable issues in a practical and helpful way.

How to Deal with Difficult People by Ursula Markham (Thorsons) is a slim paperback that offers some useful ideas on conflict management.

Planning Projects by Trevor Young (The Industrial Society) is a relatively concise book that offers step-by-step guidelines for successful project management.

Summary

Managing customer service means:

- Motivating staff to approach work positively as attitudes are very important in the customer service mix. The manager needs to:

    o build up the value of the jobs that service staff do

    o praise good work and give staff credit for their successes

    o foster a 'teamwork' approach.

- Taking special care to value the work that part-time staff do and include them in the team.

- Organizing efficient systems to deliver effective and consistent customer service at all times.

- Championing customer service within the organization to ensure that sufficient resources are allocated to this important function. This can mean building a good business case to justify additional expenditure to ensure customer loyalty.

- Promoting high standards of service by setting clear, measurable performance targets for staff.

Part 2
Specific skills and competencies

4
Overview of communication issues

Communication: methods, meaning and management

Communication is about the *sharing of a meaning*, whether it's you understanding the complaint that a customer is making, or whether it's you helping a customer to understand your organization's credit terms. The aim is the transfer of understanding.

Understanding can be more than just a sharing of knowledge. You may know that one of your products didn't turn up in time for your customer's daughter's seventh birthday. This knowledge is not the same as understanding the impact this had on your customer — the customer may feel disappointment, annoyance or even hurt. Feelings are an important part of communication which is why the chapter on face-to-face communications deals with active listening skills and the need to show empathy as well as the basic business of attending to what the customer says.

Feelings are harder to express and to detect when a person isn't in front of you — if all you have is an angry letter or a telephone message, it can be hard to understand what the problem really is. However, it is important that you demonstrate at least some interest in the other person's feelings. Business has a human face and it's vital to appear sympathetic and open to your customers' complaints, comments and enquiries.

If it is the message that matters and not the medium, why has the discussion of communication been divided into three different chapters? The answer to this lies in the detail. Techniques that work when you are talking to someone on the phone won't work in writing. Likewise, you have time to craft a written response in a way that would not be possible if you were responding to someone face to face. Each method has its benefits and its drawbacks and is more appropriate for certain sets of circumstances than others. So it's important to choose the right communication format to deliver the right message — and do it at the right time.

Sometimes, the choice of communication format or style isn't up to you — the customer may present him or herself in front of you with a question or complaint and demand an answer. If it is a long and complex matter, you can't simply tell them to go away and put it in writing — even if this would be easier for you. Instead you have to listen carefully and disentangle the main points from the surrounding issues and then start to compose your response. At that point, you may be able to suggest that you need to investigate matters further and promise to write with a full report later. But if someone is standing in front of you demanding an immediate reply, then you need to find some way of defusing the situation so that you can bring your communication skills to bear. The issue of calming down a hostile encounter is dealt with in Chapter 10.

As a manager, it is not enough for you to learn how to communicate in a wide range of situations — you also have to ensure that your staff are equally well trained and flexible in their responses. This means that you have a responsibility for ensuring that your staff have both the skills and the knowledge to be able to communicate successfully with the customers.

This may have recruitment as well as training implications. It is easier to train people to handle difficult communication problems (such as the abusive or impossibly demanding customer) if they already possess the necessary basic skills. For this reason, it may be worth setting basic written skills tests as part of your selection procedure.

We tend to assume that people know how to communicate, but perfect communication skills are rare. As a result, most people benefit from training and feedback in this area. Communication skills are essentially practical and while it's useful to discuss the underlying principles of listening, empathizing, articulating, clarifying, etc. the only way to learn to communicate in practice is to practise doing it.

Each member of the customer service team may be communicating all day long, but this is not necessarily the best way for them to learn effective skills. It may be more appropriate to organize training sessions which include role play with feedback so that everyone gets the chance to rehearse ways of dealing with likely situations and communication problems.

Feedback is a very important part of the training equation — provided that it's constructive in nature and relevant to the person hearing it. The aim of all feedback is to improve effectiveness by careful observation of existing behaviour, which helps people to become aware of and understand their current performance. This, in turn, leads them into thinking of possible improvements.

Feedback: practical guidelines

- Know the goal of your feedback — your aim is to help someone do their work better. It is important to stay focused on this outcome of feedback as otherwise negative feedback can disintegrate into generalized griping about someone's inadequate performance.

- Be specific — don't say things like 'You blew that job, didn't you?' This really doesn't help the person concerned to do better next time, it merely makes them feel bad — and while they're feeling bad, they won't be listening to your advice. Comment in detailed terms on what went right and what could be improved about the way the job was done. The more specific you are the more easily staff will be able to use your comments to alter the way they work.

- Do it immediately — give feedback as soon as possible after you have spotted something you want to comment on. It's no good waiting until the end of the week or even the end of the day. Who can remember exactly how they performed a task after a busy day has finished? The more immediate the feedback, the more effective it is.

- Give positive feedback as well as negative — negative feedback is important, but don't underestimate the importance and effectiveness of praise and encouragement. Again, keep your comments specific and immediate and you will reinforce 'good' behaviour. If you only give negative feedback then your staff will start to discount everything you say on the grounds that 'you're never satisfied with anything anyone does'.

- Criticize the performance not the performer — don't get personal and don't make generalized comments like 'You're so stupid' as this will make the other person defensive and they won't listen to anything else you say.

- Get people to 'own' their performance — encourage the other person to work with you to find better ways of doing the job. Get them involved in improving their performance and the improvements are more likely to 'stick'.

The good thing about feedback is that it is an inexpensive way of improving people's productivity and performance. It gives them the information they need to handle their job. You wouldn't drive a car without a speedometer or petrol tank gauge, yet failing to give people information about how they do their jobs is like asking them to drive without the appropriate information to guide their actions.

The communication process

The underlying process of communication is more complicated than you might at first think. This is because communication occurs on several levels and has to operate through several 'filters', all of which can distort understanding. Communication is all about getting an idea that is currently in your mind into the mind of someone else, and this requires considerable sophistication. We all learn to communicate at an early age, but this doesn't mean that it is easy nor that we all reach the same level of ability.

If you've ever heard people talking at cross-purposes or attended a meeting that has disintegrated into a series of disconnected chats, then you will know that poor communication is more confusing than no communication at all.

So how does the communication process occur? The diagram overleaf describes part of the complexity of the communication process. It shows that there are four elements to any communication process:

- the sender (i.e. the person who is trying to communicate something)
- the receiver
- the message itself
- the filters or barriers that will distort the message.

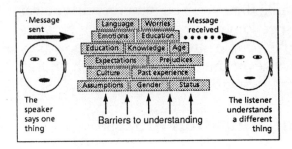

It is also important to remember that the mode of communication — spoken or written or even pictorial — will have an influence on how the message is perceived.

The next three chapters are dedicated to three different methods of communication:

* meeting a customer
* talking over the telephone
* putting things in writing.

However, whichever method you choose, the underlying aim is the same — to *understand* and to *be understood*.

5
Communication issues — face-to-face encounters

Whether it's providing information and advice, answering questions, or handling complaints, communication should ensure a two-way understanding between staff and customers so that a satisfactory result can be achieved for both customer and company.

Customer service staff typically experience a huge variety of face-to-face encounters from perhaps a two minute transaction at the checkout to a two hour meeting about a maintenance contract. Whatever the situation, there are several key factors that will always influence the outcome.

Personal approach

These days the business world is becoming more and more impersonal. There is an emphasis on time-saving and efficiency which, in many cases, is advantageous to customers and organizations alike.

Many people never meet the staff at their bank, for example, as transactions often take place on the telephone or through technology such as cash machines.

Whether you meet your customers often or rarely, it is essential to capitalize on each contact that is made. For many people, there is no substitute for the 'personal touch' which can cement a long-term relationship with the customer. There are several advantages to dealing with customers face to face:

- It is possible to form a better understanding of what the customer means and also what type of personality they are by observing their body language as well as listening to what they say.

- More time is available to explore customer needs. Unlike the telephone, meeting the customer provides a better chance to explore specific ideas. In face-to-face encounters people are not usually under so much pressure to end the conversation and this means there is more opportunity to 'delve deeper' into what the customer really thinks and feels. This may lead to the discovery of problems or queries that the customer was not aware of or had been keeping to themselves.

- Putting a face to a name often creates a personal bond between customer and company. People like to feel that they are important and valued rather than just another statistic. In fact, these days many products and services have similar features, so strong customer relationships may give your company a competitive edge.

- Visual aids and product demonstrations can be used to enhance understanding and create interest.

- Visiting a customer at their own premises will provide further insight into their needs and expectations.

Convey a professional message

Communicating face-to-face is not just about *what* is said but also about *how* it is said. The information that is conveyed should not only be correct but also be supplied by polite, friendly and efficient staff who make each customer feel valued.

As a manager, you first need to think about the overall message that your company conveys from the very moment that the customer walks through the door. It might include:

✔ We are professional

✔ We are efficient

✔ We know what we're doing

✔ We can help you

✔ We can make your life easy

✔ We are interested in you

✔ We are glad to see you

✔ We are friendly

First impressions go a long way to a satisfactory outcome so it's important that the customer feels immediately welcome rather than like an intrusive stranger. Take a step back and imagine that you are walking into your workplace for the first time. What would your first impression be? Is it a place where customers are welcomed and can easily and quickly find who or what they want or do staff view them as interruptions? Are staff trained to greet customers and point them in the right direction or do they have to find their own way around? Do staff dress appropriately for your company environment? Do you have an official receptionist? Are your premises neat and attractive?

Keys to effective communication

Once you have ensured that you are communicating the correct general message to customers then you need to look at communication on a person-to-person level. Excellent face-to-face communication is a must for an efficient customer service department and is heavily influenced by three elements:

1   Building rapport

Building and maintaining rapport is the foundation of good communication. The dictionary defines rapport as a 'harmonious and understanding relationship.' This doesn't mean that you have to be 'best buddies' with your customers but you'll achieve a better business relationship if you get to know each other on a professional level and can work comfortably together.

To achieve this goal it is essential that customers, even if they are only small accounts, feel valued by your company. This means treating them politely and respectfully as well as empathizing with their feelings. In other words, showing that their feelings are understood and that staff are willing to help them — even if the customer has made a mistake or the problem is unrelated to the service department.

Face-to-face communication helps to build rapport by creating a sense of 'personal connection'. The customer also gets a chance to assess your company through the way that staff act towards them.

With this in mind, you should ensure that your staff always act 'positively' towards your customers and are aware that their body language can either back up or belie what they say. There are several basic principles that can be applied to make customers feel welcome:

- **Smiling.** You'll probably know what it's like to approach a grumpy or unfriendly looking person. It's off-putting and sometimes intimidating — especially when you need help or are worried about something. It also gives the impression that you are somehow inconveniencing them. Bearing in mind how uncomfortable this feels, make sure that your staff greet customers with a smile on their face and a friendly attitude. Smiling is easy and goes a long way to reassuring customers that they are welcome.

- **Making eye contact.** Making eye contact with people shows them that you are interested in what they have to say and also tells them that you are confident and trustworthy. On the other hand, failing to make eye contact has several negative connotations such as lack of concentration, nervousness, shyness and untrustworthiness. For example, if a customer service representative looks away while saying that a late order will definitely arrive tomorrow, the customer may get the feeling that they are being lied to.

- **Using a firm handshake** and standing up to greet the customer is polite and indicates eagerness.

People who move energetically with their head
held up high convey confidence and enthusiasm.

- **Using an 'open' body stance.** When people are
  feeling nervous or defensive they often cross their
  arms and legs, hunch their shoulders or turn their
  bodies away from whatever is making them feel
  uncomfortable. This can often be observed in
  confrontational situations where one person is
  feeling threatened by the other. Facing the
  customer and using open palm gestures indicates
  a relaxed and confident attitude.

- **Dressing appropriately.** It's not always necessary
  to dress formally but staff should look neat and
  tidy in most cases. Even if your company dress is
  casual, smart dress should be worn for important
  customer meetings so that a professional and
  competent image is conveyed.

Read the signs

You can tell if the customer is at ease with the
conversation by observing his or her body language.
Encourage staff to look out for the following signs:

Comfort
- ✔ Maintains eye contact
- ✔ Smiles
- ✔ Nods head
- ✔ Sits forward in chair
- ✔ Demonstrates an open body stance, for example,
  leaning back in chair with hands crossed behind
  head
- ✔ Takes part in conversation, asks questions

Discomfort

✗ Averts gaze

✗ Frowns

✗ Moves away

✗ Closed body stance — crossed arms, legs

✗ Changes subject on sensitive issues

✗ Is silent and sullen

✗ Taps foot or displays others signs of nervous irritation like jigging leg or chewing pen

✗ Hand covers mouth

Observation task — do your staff make customers feel welcome?

The above principles are not difficult to apply in practice and can have an extremely positive effect on the way customers feel about your company. Try observing the way that your staff interact with customers. You won't need to hear what they are saying. Observing the body language of both staff and customers will give you a good indication of how each person feels about the other. Do your staff seem pleased to see customers or does it look like they couldn't care less? Do customers look as if they are relaxed or do they look miserable and uptight?

Tuning in to personality types helps build rapport

Building rapport has a lot to do with finding out more about what sort of person the customer is. To this end it is vital that you train staff to listen carefully to what customers say and to how they say it as well as to observe their actions.

It's important to recognize that everyone has a preferred style of communication that he or she feels most comfortable with. This means that staff will often have to adapt their own style of communication to that of each customer.

The following categories give a broad representation of different communication styles and understanding them will make effective communication easier:

People-oriented communicators

Face-to-face communication can be very effective for building rapport with this sort of person as they value and need 'people' relationships. Developing rapport entails finding ways of 'getting on with' them so that they feel liked and valued by your company. Remembering personal information like their name and their interests will make them feel special.

This sort of person won't work on logic alone. Your company may offer high-quality, competitively priced products but if they don't like the people they are dealing with they may well go elsewhere.

Business-oriented communicators

This sort of person is primarily concerned with business issues such as identifying the financial justification of any contract and ensuring that they get value for money. A good business deal is more important to them than building relationships within the company. A business-oriented person appreciates impersonal yet time-saving technology which allows them to conduct business with the company without actually having to visit the premises. This means that there is less chance of meeting them face to face so that, if anything, it is even more important to make every contact count.

This type of communicator will get irritated by small talk or 'getting to know you' attempts so the best approach is to get straight down to business and to demonstrate expertise with regard to the products and services concerned as well as the industry sector.

Technically-oriented communicators

Technical types are extremely interested in the product or service that your company provides and conversation should concentrate on this. They like to keep abreast of technical jargon, new developments and are interested in the 'nuts and bolts' of the product.

Meeting this sort of person provides an ideal opportunity to demonstrate products or services — technically-oriented people love to try things out for themselves as well as to enhance presentations through visual aids.

Extensive product knowledge is needed to communicate effectively with 'technos' as they're likely to ask lots of questions and be up-to-date on competitive product development.

Although customers don't usually fall neatly into one category or another keen observation and careful listening will provide clues to their bias. For example, a people-oriented customer will be keen to shake hands and talk about themselves whereas a technically-oriented customer will be eager to get on and examine the product or service.

How do you communicate?

People find that they don't 'hit it off' with others and this is often because their communication styles differ. It's important to recognize your own style of communication so that you can view situations more objectively and gain a better understanding of customers. For example, Susannah, a PR consultant, works on a large confectionery account which is highly profitable for her company. Despite this, Susannah dislikes dealing with the company's account manager as she feels that he is a 'difficult' person. In her opinion, he is brusque bordering on rude and always fails to respond to her sociable attempts at 'breaking the ice' with 'polite' conversation.

At the next client meeting:

Client: 'I'll say straight off that I'm pleased with the way that the campaign is going and happy that it hasn't gone over budget. However, I think it's a waste of time meeting every month and from now on we should only meet when it's necessary to hammer out new ideas. We've got a new launch in July and we're thinking of using you for the campaign.'

Susannah: 'It's nice to meet up and talk over the relevant issues and I hope that you're happy with the service we're providing.'

Client: 'Yes.'

Susannah: 'And will the account director still want to meet up every month?'

Client: 'That's up to him.'

Susannah: 'Would it be easier if I came to your offices?'

In this scenario, Susannah who is people-oriented fails to recognize that her style of communication needs to be adapted to a business-/technically-oriented style. This means that she is concerned with 'getting on' with the client rather than concentrating on the business side of the relationship which, for the client, is of paramount importance and which he is happy with. It also means that she fails to follow up on an opening for future business.

2   Active listening

Another crucial skill for effective communication to take place is active listening. This may seem obvious but there is a big difference between hearing what is being said and actually taking in the meaning of the conversation so that a true and objective understanding of the situation can be achieved. Active listening is often hampered by various factors which can lead to misunderstandings and mistakes.

Many people are bad listeners and can get the wrong end of the stick. Have you ever spent several minutes listening to somebody only to realize that you haven't a clue what they've said? This can be costly for your company and cause the customer unnecessary delays and irritation. It's a good idea to review how you and your team listen to your customers. Do you always get a full and clear picture on which to base your answers?

For many, active listening does not come naturally and needs to be learned and developed. The following points are central to active listening:

Attend to what the customer is saying

It is important to concentrate fully on what is being said throughout every customer interaction no matter how straightforward the situation may seem initially. This is more difficult than it sounds: when people are busy or under pressure their minds often wander to things that seem more important. It's also easy to become distracted by interruptions from colleagues or from background noise.

Even if people think they can do two things at once, distracted listening results in opinions being formed on the basis of a partially attended exchanges. This usually leads to misunderstandings and unnecessary

errors which inconvenience both the customer and
company.

When people are distracted they often rush the
speaker through what they are saying so that they can
get on with what they really want to do. Or they make
up their minds about what the speaker is trying to say
without really listening to the facts and attend only to
the information that confirms or supports their
immediate opinion. When this happens, people are
likely to make false assumptions and jump to
incorrect conclusions from what they *think* they've
heard.

Being objective

It can be difficult to form an accurate opinion as many
people, perhaps unconsciously, are heavily influenced
by their own views and feelings. This sometimes
results in passing judgement before much, if
anything, has been said.

Judgemental listening is often based on things like
accents and appearance. It is important to learn to
listen without any preconceptions, otherwise the
listener may come across as rude, hostile or
patronizing. This can lead to misunderstandings,
disputes or aggression and eventually to the loss of a
customer.

Understanding the customer's feelings

Just like building rapport, active listening includes
showing customers that their point of view is
recognized and understood. Phrases such as: 'I can
understand how you feel...', 'Go on...' and 'I see what
you mean...' encourage customers to voice their side
of the story.

Paraphrasing to check meaning

A good way to check that there is a clear and complete understanding of what is being said is for the listener to translate the message into their own words (paraphrase) and then repeat it back to the speaker. This gives the speaker a chance to confirm or correct the listener *before* errors are made. For example:

Customer: 'I think I'm going to be made redundant. There have been a lot of rumours flying around the office lately. My wife is very worried that we won't be able to keep up with the mortgage repayments. Just last week one of my colleagues was given his marching orders — after twenty years! Can you believe it? Anyway, that's not your problem.'
Customer service representative: 'It sounds like you're worried that you won't be able to keep up with the mortgage repayments.'

Asking questions to find out more information

It's possible to draw out further details and clarify understanding by asking questions. It's sometimes necessary to be tentative about this to encourage open rather than defensive answers. The speaker should avoid sounding too abrupt and explain why he or she needs the information if appropriate. Questions fall into three broad categories:

- *Open questions.* These questions begin with who, what, when, where and how, and are intended to draw out more information. For example, 'What happened?' Open questions prevent the discussion taking on the form of an interrogation as they invite the customer to talk in depth about what's concerning them.

- *Probing questions.* This sort of question asks for more specific details and can help to focus the customer on important points in the conversation. For example, 'What happened after you'd phoned us to let us know that your delivery was late?'

- *Closed questions.* This sort of question asks the customer to confirm or deny a point. For example, 'Did you write to us to say you'd changed address?'

Summarizing to clarify understanding

When the speaker has finished what he or she has to say, it is a good idea for the listener to briefly summarize the main points of the conversation to confirm that both the speaker and listener understand one another.

Taking notes to remember important points

Writing down crucial points in the conversation helps to ensure that they are remembered accurately. Customers should be encouraged to write down important points too, and to ask questions about anything of which they are unsure.

3 Making a response

Once a clear understanding of the customer's situation is obtained, the next step to effective communication is to make an accurate and informed response. Your staff need to be well trained in product knowledge and company procedures to be able to make a prompt and correct response.

Time, effort and inconvenience will be saved if a correct response is given at the first attempt — even if this means asking the customer to wait for an answer. If there is a necessary delay in replying, it is important to explain what is happening to the customer and make a commitment to give them an answer by a specific time: 'That's an interesting question and I'll have to check into it to give you a correct answer. I'll let you know by ten o'clock tomorrow morning.'

The response should be concise and focus on the customer's enquiry. It is a good idea to stop after each main point of the answer to check that the customer has understood what is being said. It is essential to articulate clearly and speak at a pace that customers can understand.

Team task

Listening, understanding and remembering what customers say can be a challenging task so give your staff plenty of opportunity to practise their listening skills:

- Ask your team to divide themselves into groups of three: one person will act the part of the customer service representative, one the customer and one the observer.

- Invent role play scenarios. Include some complicated points and figures that will test the customer service representative's memory. Encourage the customers to get into their parts by perhaps displaying their emotions, waffling on etc.

- Ask the observer to give constructive feedback on the customer service representative's performance as well as coming up with some positive suggestions for improvement.

- Swap everyone around so that each member has a chance to play each part.

- Gather the team together to discuss the most important points that each group learned from the exercise.

- Use the section on active listening to coach your team in listening skills.

Staff empowerment

To ensure consistency and accuracy most companies
have standard information to meet customer requests.
However, to increase efficiency and to meet
individual customer needs, your staff need to be
given the responsibility to make spontaneous,
informed decisions which may not strictly adhere to
company policy but will result in adding value to the
business by perhaps retaining or gaining a customer.
For example:

Customer: 'How long would I have to settle my
account if I were to go ahead with the order?'
Customer service representative: 'You need to pay within
30 days.'
C: 'Well, my budget doesn't come through until the
end of the month so I'll need 40 days if I'm going to
go ahead. If I'm pleased with what I get I might even
make a regular order.'
CSR: 'Well, I don't know if that's possible. I'll have to
ask my manager when she gets back from lunch.
Could you drop in later on this afternoon?'

In this case, the employee has no decision-making
authority which not only causes inconvenience to the
customer but also means that the company may lose a
new order. Even if the manager agrees to an extra ten
days' leeway on payment, it might be too late as the
customer may have gone elsewhere.

The amount of responsibility that you give your
staff will depend on a number of factors:

* **Relevant experience** — junior members of staff
  will be less able to make informed decisions than
  more senior members. However, many companies
  have found that empowering even junior members

to some extent encourages them to feel responsible and also results in a higher standard of customer service. Empowering staff may lead to some mistakes but these are outweighed by benefits such as efficiency, immediacy, customer satisfaction and also motivated staff who feel that they have a say in what they do.

Team task

It's a good idea to review your face-to-face communication effectiveness on a regular basis. Team discussions will not only serve to sharpen skills but also throw up some new ideas on where and how improvements can be made.

- Ask your team what they think the most important elements in face-to-face communication are.

- Before the session begins, ask one or two of your team to observe the others' body language. At the end of half an hour ask them to share what they have observed with the rest of the team. This exercise is meant to allow people to see what sort of impression they give even when they unaware of it.

- Discuss communication styles. First ask each person to pinpoint their own style and then ask for the rest of the team's comments. Objective observations can be very useful in helping people to see how they really act.

- Ask your staff to summarize the content of your training session — this will show if they have listened, understood and remembered what has been said. In other words, if they are effective face-to-face communicators.

- **Customer history** — if a lucrative long-term customer asks a favour then it is likely to be advantageous to the company in the long run as the customer is more likely to remain loyal in the future. Remember that 'excellent customer service' can only be defined by the customer and this may mean changing to fit an individual customer's expectation in some cases. However, it is important to keep track of 'favours'. Too much generosity may eat into profit margins unless the customer 'gives' as much as he or she 'takes'.

- **Potential business** — if there is the possibility of obtaining a large account then it is often necessary 'to strike while the iron is hot'.

Summary

The ability to communicate well helps your staff increase their performance levels and provide a better standard of customer service. Making personal contact and completing a successful transaction in which both customer and staff member are satisfied can also be a rewarding and enjoyable part of the customer service role.

- Face-to-face contact with customers can cement long-term business relationships. With so many similar products on the market, strong relationships can mean the difference between retaining or losing the customer.

- First impressions count so make sure that your company conveys a professional image.

- Effective communication should ensure a two-way understanding between customer and company. It depends on active listening, building rapport and well thought out responses.

- Different communication styles can enhance or hamper understanding. Your staff should be aware of how they communicate and be able to adapt their style to match each customer.

- Empowering staff to make decisions improves communication and provides a more efficient service for the customer.

6
Communication issues — using the telephone

Whether you work for a small company or a large organization, the telephone provides a vital link between you and your customers and is a popular and widespread method of business communication. The telephone can be a powerful communication tool if used correctly. Consider its advantages over other forms of communication:

- **Convenient.** It's often easier and more immediate for both customers and staff to carry out transactions over the telephone.

- **Time-saving.** Many people who can spare a five minute phone call would be hard pushed to take an hour out of their day to call in to your premises. Even if customers need to deal with the company face to face for the main business transaction the telephone makes it easy to provide further information and deal with questions and queries.

- **Cost-effective.** It's cheaper to use the telephone than to arrange to travel to a face-to-face meeting.

- **Easy to monitor.** You can closely monitor the quality of your staff's calls.

- **More productive.** More customers can be dealt with in a shorter space of time.

In many ways communicating over the telephone is more difficult than dealing with customers face to face. Visual clues are an important element in gaining a two-way understanding of what is being said and play a large part in building rapport. There is also less time to recover from mistakes and talk issues through. Because of this, it is particularly important that you spend time developing your staff's telephone manner to ensure that they communicate effectively. If the telephone is meant to make things easier for the customer, it's up to you to ensure that it is exactly what it does.

Dealing with incoming calls

Before you think about what your staff are saying to customers you should set about establishing an efficient system by which your customers can easily get through to the person to whom they wish to speak. First impressions count and when using the phone there are only a few seconds to show that you are a professional organization which values its customers. Set the right tone from the very beginning of the conversation by ensuring that your staff adhere to the following steps:

- Answer promptly. Business is frequently lost because of an unanswered telephone. The ideal time to pick up the receiver is within four rings. Studies show that if the telephone isn't answered by the fifth ring, callers get the impression that your company is inefficient. After six to eight rings, most callers give up. Let's face it, if you can't organize yourselves to pick up the telephone then how can you be trusted to deal with more important business issues?

- Welcome customers politely. There's no excuse for being rude or impatient when answering the telephone. Can you imagine how off-putting it would be if you smiled and offered to shake hands on meeting a person and, rather than greeting you in the same way, they turned their back on you? This is what it feels like for callers who are not greeted with courtesy and warmth.

  An unwelcoming attitude can irritate or unnerve the customer unnecessarily. This often makes the ensuing conversation difficult or uncomfortable as the customer is left with the impression that your company does not really want to hear from them.

- Answer the telephone with an enthusiastic and cheerful tone that says: 'We are pleased to hear from you and we want to help you.' This is not difficult to achieve and can make a huge difference to the way that customers feel about your company.

- Provide information. Customers need to know that they are through to the right company/person/ department. For example, 'Good morning, customer service, how can I help you?' Robotic responses should be avoided as they give the impression that the customer is just one more call to add to the hundreds that have already been taken that day. Even if the content of the response is correct but it is said in an unfriendly way, it will convey an uncaring message to customers. Whether computer records are available at each work-station or information is supplied in written form, it should be easily accessible so that quick and accurate responses can be given to customer enquiries.

- Help customers contact the correct person easily. If the customer doesn't get through to the right person at once, it's essential that the person they do speak to spends time to help them make contact. Answers like: 'They're not here, you'll have to ring back later,' may save the service representative's time in the short run but could end up losing the customer.

  Team work and a common goal — to provide excellent customer service for all customers — are particularly useful in this sort of situation. If the right person cannot be located then the member of staff should offer to deal with the enquiry if they can. If this is not possible, then the customer should be assured that the right person will call them back within a given time limit.

- Take messages. Messages should be taken down accurately and passed on to the correct person promptly. All messages should provide the customer's name and telephone number and a brief summary of the customer's enquiry.

  If messages don't reach the required destination, the customer may be forced to call back, which at best is inefficient and irritating and at worst may mean that the person who didn't receive the message must deal with an angry customer on the next contact. If the message is inaccurate or isn't taken down at all, the customer will be required to repeat or clarify his or her original enquiry which suggests that your company suffers from poor internal communication.

Room for improvement

A recent survey found that out of 3,000 calls made to various sized companies:

- Over 50 per cent were greeted by an unfriendly sounding person.

- Over 35 per cent of the calls rang more that six times and only 1 per cent received an apology for being kept waiting.

For callers who were put through to the right extension:

- Over 40 per cent were kept waiting while the right person was located and very few received apologies for being kept waiting.

- Over 44 per cent who asked to be called back by someone who could provide answers to their query were not contacted again.

If you think that this sort of thing could never happen in your company then try this experiment: Call in from an outside line with a tricky request. Give a name that's hard to pronounce and spell, and then ask to speak to someone who can help you solve your problem. If they have to call you back don't offer to give your telephone number.
You may be surprised at how easy it is to lose a customer.
Try this exercise on a regular basis. If you have worked at achieving high standards, it would be a shame to slip back into bad habits.

Outgoing calls

Just like incoming calls, outgoing calls need to convey a clear and professional message. Outgoing calls should be initiated with an introduction of who is calling, the name of your organization and the reason for the call. For example, 'Hello Mrs Walters, this is Tom Smith from Welco. I am calling about the invoice query that you made this morning.'

To save time and convey the correct message, it is important to plan the call beforehand. This may only take a few seconds — perhaps to read over written notes or a computer file — or several minutes to consider a difficult problem and the best ways of handling it.

Deciding on the objective of the call beforehand not only stops the caller waffling and confusing the customer, but also enables the caller to take more control of the call which reduces the possibility of failing to get the message over.

Difficult calls

No matter how well your staff handle telephone communication, there will always be some difficult customers to deal with or complicated problems to solve.

The main point to remember is that when problems arise they should always be dealt with at the earliest opportunity. In particular, telling the customer that 'someone will call back...' and then hoping that the problem will go away just doesn't work (even though it is a popular ploy with some companies).

Initiating a call gives the customer service representative a psychological advantage and gives them the time to prepare what they are going to say. This makes it less likely that they will be caught off guard by an irritated customer who has had to call back. It also shows the customer that your company is willing to make the effort to put things right if something has gone wrong.

The caller should be prepared to put up with some hostility if your company has inconvenienced the customer. But, an empathic attitude and a willingness to sort out the problem should take the heat out of the

situation. (See Chapter 9 on complaint handling and
Chapter 10 on handling difficult customers.)

**What customers hate when they telephone
organizations**

- **Being left on hold with no explanation**

  Don't abandon callers to the automated hold music or
  worse, the silence of a line in limbo. If you have to put a
  caller on hold, keep checking with them that they don't
  mind waiting a bit longer. If they don't want to hold, tell
  them the person they need to ask for next time they call
  or take their number and arrange for someone to call
  them back.

- **Being passed from pillar to post**

  It can be difficult in a large organization to identify
  whom the customer should be speaking to but nobody
  likes being passed from department to department and
  having to tell their story all over again each time. Have a
  list of contacts for frequent enquires so you can put
  customers through to the right person first time.

- **Having to listen to data being entered on to the
  computer**

  You may have to type information into your system to
  answer the customer's query but it is polite to tell them
  what you're doing and apologize for keeping them
  waiting if your system is slow to respond or if you have
  to enter a lot of data. Make the occasional comment
  along the lines of: 'Sorry to keep you waiting, I'm just
  entering your password on to the database so that I can
  check the balance of your account, it won't take a
  minute... Yes, it's going through the system now.'

Leaving messages

It can be hard work getting hold of some people on
the telephone. Even when they are keen to hear from
your company, the pressure of their work ties them
up in meetings, keeps them on the phone to other
people or sends them out of the office on urgent
appointments.

A recent survey in one large computer organization found that people only received 38 per cent of their phone calls personally — the rest of the calls were either handled by someone else taking a message or by the voice mail system.

That's why it's essential to be prepared to leave a clear message whenever calling a customer. Leaving a clear message will be easier when callers:

- Know why they're calling so they can leave a concise and informative message.

- Speak slowly and clearly.

- Make sure the message tells customers what is needed so that they can find the appropriate information before calling back.

Keys to effective telephone communication

Just like face-to-face communication, successfully dealing with customers over the telephone depends on effective questioning, active listening, building rapport and clear and accurate responses (see Chapter 5). However, it can be more difficult over the telephone because, as has been mentioned, gaining understanding is limited to listening and speaking. This means that skills need to be even sharper for excellent results to be achieved.

If your department's telephone calls are put through the company reception, it is vital that receptionists are trained in good telephone techniques too. They are sometimes excluded from training courses and not regarded as customer service staff. However, receptionists and other 'support' staff are often the first people whom a customer calling into your company speaks to and can have a big impact on customers' first impressions.

Including support staff in appropriate training sessions increases skills and motivation. People are inspired to do better if they feel that they are a valued member of the team rather that 'just the person who answers the phone'.

Voice power

When dealing with customers face to face, building rapport often relies on visual signs such as eye contact and smiling whereas on the telephone the ability to strike up a comfortable bond with customers depends to a great extent on the voice. For this reason it is particularly important to work on the way your staff sound on the telephone. The pace, tone, pronunciation and volume of a person's voice can build up a vivid picture in the customer's mind. Your aim is to ensure that your customers think of your staff as confident, competent and friendly rather than timid little mice or overbearing battle-axes. Consider the three 'Ps' of voice power:

- **Pace.** Speaking too quickly may indicate lack of confidence or nervousness as well as making it more difficult for the listener to understand what is said. Speaking too slowly gives the impression that the speaker isn't sure of what they are talking about and can lose the listener's interest. Speakers should aim to keep a steady pace but when a point needs to be emphasized, a good device is to speed up or to slow down. 'Punching out' key phrases in each sentence also helps the listener to focus on the main points.

- **Pitch.** A deeper tone sounds more confident than a higher one. High-pitched voices tend to sound child-like and also belie nervousness or agitation. This is not to say that you should encourage your staff to speak with a monotonous tone: raising or lowering pitch is a good way of making delivery more interesting. The voice tends to sound flatter over the telephone, so more emphasis needs to be placed on sounding enthusiastic than would be needed in a face-to-face situation.

- **Pronunciation.** Many people find regional accents attractive. However, what's most important is articulation, especially on technical words or complicated points so that the speaker can be easily understood.

Tips for building telephone rapport

✔ **Cheerfulness** — no one likes dealing with miserable people.

✔ **Politeness** — courtesy costs nothing and is a habit that can easily be acquired.

✔ **Patience** — show empathy to customers even when they are wrong. Take the time to explain things again.

✔ **Sensitivity** — extra sensitivity is needed to listen for the way the customer is feeling.

✔ **Professionalism** — personal feelings should not get in the way of meeting customer demand.

✔ **Enthusiasm** — the voice sounds flatter over the telephone so it's important to smile and make an extra effort to sound friendly and excited about what you're saying.

Team task

The best way to help your staff to improve their voices is to let them listen to how they sound for themselves. If possible, use real-life recordings of their telephone conversations. If this is not possible ask your staff to record themselves speaking with a colleague.

Ask each person to consider the following questions when they listen to the recordings:

- Am I speaking too quickly to be clearly understood or so slowly I might lose the customer's interest?
- Did I sound confused or unsure because my voice was too high?
- Did I speak clearly so that my words could be understood?
- Did I speak too softly or too loudly?
- Did I sound friendly?
- Did I sound enthusiastic?

Try to make this exercise fun as people are often embarrassed by their own voices and won't be open to learning new techniques if they feel stupid.

Gaining a clear understanding

Unfortunately, you cannot train your customers to be better communicators and this is why it is so important to spend some time and effort improving your staff's style of communication when using the telephone.

Concentration, empathy, paraphrasing and asking questions as discussed in the previous chapter are all just as relevant to gaining a clear understanding over the telephone (see Chapter 5). However, some points are particularly important when talking on the telephone:

- **Concentration.** It is easier to get distracted or to try to do another task when using the telephone because the customer cannot see what is happening. Doing two things at the same time or even carrying out two conversations at once (you often see people mouthing things to colleagues when they are talking to someone else on the telephone) is one of the main causes of mistakes and misunderstandings.

- **Clarifying understanding.** It's often harder to understand or to be understood over the telephone, especially when talking about complicated or technical subjects. It's also easy to lose track of what customers are saying, especially while attempting to write down important points. The only way you can tell if the customer understands is by what they say and the tone of their voice. Be alert to sounds of unease or tentativeness on the part of the customer as this may indicate that he or she has not understood what has been said but doesn't like to admit it.

- **Check the whole story.** Although it's tempting to get the gist of what's been said and try to sort out the details later, this can lead to misunderstandings. It's better to stop the customer and ask them to repeat or rephrase what they've said as, although this takes longer in the short term, it saves the time that would be needed to correct mistakes in the long term. Always paraphrase difficult or important topics to check the meaning. Patience and double-checking are needed, especially with customers who have difficulty in speaking English.

- **Concise questions.** There are usually time constraints when using the telephone, so there's less chance to chat through issues. This means that questions need to be more focused and concise so that it's possible to get to the heart of the matter more quickly.

Detect a change of mood

It's usually easy to detect an angry customer — they sound angry and they say they're angry! However, in some circumstances the customer may become upset for a reason that is difficult to pinpoint. If this happens, it's important to empathize with the customer and defuse the emotional situation so that you can both think logically about the matter at hand.

Listen for signs of customer agitation:

- Raised voice
- More rapid speech
- Less clear pronunciation
- Higher pitch
- The customer says less and less
- Shouting!

Case study — putting the telephone to work

As a telecommunications company, Orange has put the phone at the heart of its customer service programme. The management team has worked hard to create a culture in which customers feel that the care and advice they receive is specifically tailored to meet their individual needs. This is a big challenge given that the company has 930,000 customers throughout the UK and is growing at approximately 45,000 customers per month.

The company receives around 25,000 calls per day which include new customers wishing to register, people wanting help and advice, and complaints. It aims to answer all calls within 20 seconds and whenever possible to make what it describes as 'first call resolutions'.

Staff are multi-skilled so that they can deal with any type of call. This means that customers can be dealt with immediately even if they have several queries which might cross departmental boundaries. This is more efficient and convenient for both company and customer.

Each customer service operator is equipped with a computer so that customer information is easily accessible. Headsets enable operators to use their computers easily while talking on the phone.

The company is aware that customer service has a personal element and although it aims to deal with as many calls as possible, it recognizes the error of sacrificing quality for quantity. For example, the registration department's staff work from scripts which prompt them to ask for all essential details but they are free to chat (to build rapport) with the customer if they think it is appropriate.

Investment in technological development has made it easier for staff to help customers on their first contact. For example, each member of staff on the help desk has access to a computer package which helps them sort out customer queries and problems: if a customer rings in and says that they have a handset problem, for example, the service representative just types in 'handset' problem' and a list of relevant questions comes up on the screen. The process helps the service representative to narrow down, pinpoint and possibly redefine the problem; at which point the right solution for that customer can be supplied.

Developing a customer care system that suits your company

Whether you work for a telephone-based operation or not, the telephone is an essential communication medium. Even if you work for a small company which is unable to afford a large amount of investment into your system you will be able to adapt much of the Orange philosophy to improve your own outfit. Look at Orange's criteria to improve its customer service below and see if you can pinpoint ways to improve yours as a result.

- **Customer service is available 24 hours a day, 365 days a year** — if you do not have the resources for this, you can at least provide an answering machine to allow customers to leave messages and to say when a member of staff will next be able to contact them. Depending on the type of business, it may be worth developing a rota where one member of staff can be contacted in an emergency.

- **Staff strive to offer first call resolution** — your company may not be able to stretch to advanced technology but it's still possible to develop a system which enables customers to be dealt with quickly and efficiently. Whether stored on a computer or in note form, make sure that departmental and customer documentation is easily accessible, up-to-date and accurate. If possible, ensure that staff are multi-skilled so that, when necessary, each person can deal with any query or problem that they come up against.

- **Written queries and those not resolved on the first call are resolved with 48 hours** — the quicker you are able to provide customers with the answers they require the more likely you are to gain or hold on to their business. Estimate a resolution time that is suitable for your department and make sure that your staff are aware of the required time limit. You may find that you can reasonably expect all queries to be resolved within a few hours.

- **All customer calls from handsets are free** — free phone services are a way of adding value to the product and 'giving something back' to customers. If your company does not provide a free phone option then it is probably even more important that an efficient service is provided. Customers will feel aggrieved if time and money is wasted on 'ringing back' or 'holding on.'

- **Ninety per cent of calls answered within 20 seconds** — encourage all staff to take responsibility for a prompt answering service.

- **Jargon minimized through use of plain English** — this is a must for effective communication through any chosen medium. Staff should avoid technical jargon and ensure that both caller and listener understand what is being said.

- **Responses are made via the customer's chosen communication medium** — e.g. email, fax, call, letter. It is important to make customer transactions as easy and comfortable as possible. Remember that what's most efficient for your company may not always fit in with customer expectations.

Summary

The telephone is such a normal part of everyday life that most people don't give a second thought to whether they are using it to its best effect. Research outlined in this chapter indicates that many companies have yet to master telecommunication and may be losing many customers as a result. As a manager, you can't afford to overlook your staff's telephone skills so don't delay in giving a performance overview and providing training in weak areas. Remember that:

- Communicating over the telephone should be quick, easy and convenient. It is essential to set an efficient answering system so that your customers can easily get through to the person they wish to speak to.

- Calls should be answered promptly by polite and friendly staff.

- Planning before making outgoing calls saves time and confusion.

- Messages should be clear and concise.

- It can be more difficult to gain a clear understanding of the customer's needs when using the phone. This means that developing communication skills such as careful listening, questioning and clear pronunciation are extremely important.

- It is worth spending time on training all support staff in telephone techniques as good communications promote better working relationships with customers at every level.

Kirby LRC

Middlesbrough College

Roman Road

Middlesbrough

TS5 5PJ

7
Communication issues — putting it in writing

Why bother?

The telephone is such an easy and immediate form of communication that you may wonder why should you bother to write to your customers? However, there are a number of good reasons for putting things in writing:

- It puts information on the record and this is relevant if there is any possibility of further dispute.

- Some customers prefer to receive information in writing — it gives them more confidence in its credibility or more time to absorb its meaning.

- Writing information out often helps to clarify the meaning so that the end result is a clearer form of communication — and there is less chance of a misunderstanding arising.

- It's quicker than phoning people who are hard to reach and it has the advantage of being cheaper too.

- It's more convenient for the customer who can read the letter when he or she chooses rather than being interrupted by a phone call.

- You can create 'standard' documents on your word processors and use them in response to common enquiries — this cuts down on writing time and effort and ensures a consistency of response.

Standards

As a manager, one of your chief concerns about written communications is to ensure that they consistently meet high standards. Many of the general points listed below should apply to all your written communications — even the more informal ones.

If you are concerned that your staff will not be able to write good letters then you need to set up a series of standard letters and train your staff in the art of clearly written communication. The list below should help you to explain to your employees what you expect from a letter or fax. There is no real excuse for sending out sloppy or misspelt letters — it's the equivalent of turning up for a meeting with a customer in a pair of ripped jeans and a T-shirt. Presentation does count and your customers will judge you on your performance in this area — especially since they have ample time to examine your letters or faxes carefully.

In fact, excellent written communications can differentiate you from your competitors as the sad truth is that far too many companies either do not exercise sufficient control over their letters or employ people who lack the basic skills and therefore cannot produce good quality letters. This problem is not restricted to small or unknown businesses, some household names are also guilty of sending out unprofessional or ill-thought-out letters.

Here are some general points to be aware of for effective written communications — for brevity the points all refer to 'letters' but these points can be generally applied to any kind of written communication.

- Before starting to write, ask yourself: 'What am I trying to achieve by writing this letter? Am I conveying information, answering a question, expressing an apology, or promoting a particular product or service?' If you don't have the core idea clearly in your mind when you start writing, then there's little chance of your being able to express it to the reader.

- Keep letters as short as possible. Don't get pompous and flowery just because you are writing it down. Don't 'pad' letters out. Avoid phrases like 'I am writing with regard to your letter,' as it's obvious that you are writing. Try saying, 'Thank you for your letter.'

- Write in plain English. Words like 'heretofore' and 'in reference to' may be suitable for solicitors but they confuse most people and don't add any meaning, so avoid using them.

- Get the personal details of the addressee correct — the misspelling of names is a particular source of irritation for customers, especially if it persists despite their requests for corrections (this tends to

happen if you use databases and don't update
your records).

- Ensure that letters are grammatically correct —
  avoid using lots of subordinate clauses which tend
  to lead to error and confusion. Keep sentences
  short and grammatically simple.

- Keep each element of the letter short — short
  sentences in short paragraphs. Try to express only
  one idea per paragraph.

- If you have a number of short points to express
  then put them in a list, indented from the main
  text.

- Include all the necessary information to respond to
  the customer's enquiry or complaint. Ideally you
  only want to write one letter, so marshal your facts
  before you begin to write.

- Use polite and courteous language — remember
  that a letter will be read 'cold' by the customer and
  any harsh or aggressive phrases will look much
  worse in black and white than if they were spoken
  with a smile direct to the customer's face. Never
  use sarcasm in a written document — it can so
  easily backfire and be taken at face value.

- Spell out any acronyms and avoid jargon. You
  want documents to be as easy to understand as
  possible.

- Sign letters personally — don't 'pp' them or write
  'dictated by... and signed in his/her absence' as it looks
  impersonal and undermines the value of the letter.

- Spell-check every letter without fail. Word
  processing systems make it easy for a document to
  be completely correct, so use this valuable facility.

- Read every letter before signing it — spell-checkers do have their drawbacks and can let some real howlers through simply because they are real words (just not the ones you intended). Also spell-checkers can suggest some entertaining replacements for unknown words so if you don't pay attention, you can get some unfortunate substitutions.

- If you have written a 'difficult' letter (especially one where you feel angry about the subject) — perhaps in response to a complaint, then put it on one side and read it again later in the day when you feel less annoyed about the issue. It is better to read such letters 'cold' to make sure that you haven't gone over the top or missed out a vital fact.

- Ensure that letters are cleanly and neatly presented — line up margins with letterhead and check that standard letters are designed to ensure that the address appears in the right place for use with 'window' envelopes and that they don't 'run over' the page by one or two lines.

- Make sure that everyone in your department uses the same font for letters to ensure a consistency of appearance. With word processors, it's tempting to 'play' with lots of different formats and fonts, but this will lead to a hotchpotch. Define a standard and stick to it.

- Define standard letters and standard paragraphs to be inserted into non-standard letters. This saves time and encourages consistency — make sure everyone is using the standards.

- Finally, if you promise to enclose something with a letter, ensure that you do.

These general points can be applied to any kind of written correspondence. However, there are some points which are particularly relevant to letters and faxes and these are dealt with in the following sections. Email is dealt with in Chapter 8.

Letters

A lot of customer service managers think only of letters as ways of dealing with complaints — and it's true these are often the letters that will take the most time and effort to draft. But the majority of letters relate to answering ordinary enquiries, generating additional orders and promoting new services or products. Letters can and should be used to *develop* a long-term relationship as well as to *repair* one when something has gone wrong.

Team task

A useful group activity is to work together as a team to write the most positive letter you can imagine about the services your organization provides. The letter should be no more than one page of letterhead long and should communicate at least three benefits that you offer your customers.

The aim of this activity is to motivate your staff by encouraging them to focus on positive aspects of your organization, and to improve the letter-writing skills of the weaker members of your team by getting them to work with more skilled letter writers. Writing is a practical task that can only be improved through practice.

Where appropriate the end result can be used in a mailshot to existing customers who have not ordered from you lately.

When to write a letter

Letters are still very popular despite the increasing use of telecommunications. The Royal Mail delivers 18 million letters a year, and around 16 million of these are business-related. Letters may be in response to a customer contact — perhaps an enquiry for a brochure, or they can be part of a company's relationship building programme with its customers.

Letters are relatively cheap to produce and can maintain contact with customers — reminding them of an organization's goods or services. They can inform about new products, new prices, special promotions, discount rates, or new contact names.

Many letters are produced as part of a company's direct mail effort and may be written and produced *en masse* by the marketing department. However, others — especially ones directed at current or recent customers may be the direct responsibility of the customer service department.

Standard letters

The advent of word processors has made the development of standard letters particularly time-saving. There is no longer any need to retype every letter laboriously. Instead you can afford to spend time creating really effective letters to suit common situations and then just top and tail them with the customer's details. This can be done via mail-merging or using database-generated information.

It is worth spending considerable effort on creating standard letters that are clear, attractive and easy to understand. This effort will be repaid by increased customer comprehension.

The danger of using standard letters is that they can become a knee-jerk response to any and every enquiry, and sometimes it pays to take the time and trouble to respond to individuals personally. It is exceptionally irritating to receive a letter that looks nice but doesn't actually deal with any of the points the customer originally raised. Standard letters may cover 80 per cent of all the enquiries you receive, but this still leaves 20 per cent that need to be dealt with in a more thoughtful fashion.

Useful team task

You probably already have a selection of standard letters that have accumulated over the years. It would be a good idea to review them, improve them where possible, update them in the light of changing circumstances and make them consistent with each other. You can either delegate this activity to your best letter writer, or you can use this task as the basis of a team-building exercise in which you all work together to produce a set of suitable standard letters.

There are several aspects to this task, so it is possible to split your team into smaller groups to work on each element separately (so that everyone gets a chance to have some input) and then bring them all together for a final review to ensure consistency.

1 Bring the team together and discuss what are the most common enquiries from customers that could be dealt with by standard responses. Don't be tied by existing letters.

2 Hammer out the 'key messages' you want to get across to every customer — what are the points that you really want to drive home in every letter you send out?

3 Work as a team to develop some 'key sentences or phrases' that reflect the messages you have identified.

4 Allocate particular letters to small groups or pairs of employees and ask them to go away and come back with good quality drafts of these letters.

5 Gather in these drafts and circulate them around the team so that everyone gets a chance to read and comment on everyone else's work.

6 Final group meeting: discuss the letters and agree changes. Agree a consistent 'look and feel' to letters (typeface, type size, page settings, sign-off line, text alignment etc.)

7 Make sure that the new set of standard letters are loaded on every computer in the department and are being properly used.

8 Meet again to review success of new letters after a couple of months — implement any changes that are necessary.

Checking staff's correspondence

Individual replies can lead to errors and comments that do not meet your organization's objectives. This is why some managers make it a practice to check their employees' correspondence before it is sent out. However, this adds to the manager's workload and gives the impression that he or she doesn't trust his or her staff. The key to ensuring that all correspondence is acceptable is setting clear objectives and guidelines, and making sure that all staff have the necessary basic writing skills to carry out their tasks.

Credit control correspondence

Correspondence for the purpose of chasing up customer payment is a very specific form of communication with customers and because it deals with the potentially 'difficult' subject of money, such correspondence requires particular care. Credit control may or may not lie within your departmental remit, but even if it is dealt with by the accounts department, you may want to have some input into the sort of letters that are sent to late-paying customers.

Chasing for payment can be a 'touchy' area for customer relations, particularly when dealing with individuals rather than other businesses. It is worth spending some time to devise an effective but non-threatening letter campaign to encourage timely payment. Some companies move straight from a bill to a 'threatening letter' if payment isn't received by the due date. Others find it more appropriate to send reminder letters to late payers. Customer care manager, Gwilym Roberts, told *The Times* that Barclaycard has been encouraging its managers to adopt a more conversational tone in the letters they send to customers and that research has show that this style change has been appreciated. Late payers of Barclaycard accounts are sent a brief reminder which points out the outstanding balance on their account and asks them politely to call a customer service person to discuss the issue and prevent the account being closed. Barclaycard wants the letter to be firm enough to encourage action but without offending genuinely forgetful customers.

Team task: *Create a 'friendly' chasing letter for your late payers*

Simply reading and correcting other people's correspondence is a waste of managerial time. You may need to check correspondence occasionally, but you do want to be able to trust your staff to write effective and professional letters. So when you check letters be sure to explain to staff how you think they could be improved.

The aim is to coach staff in letter writing and set clear standards of acceptability for them. Any correspondence that does not meet the standards you have set should be done again by the person concerned until they get it right — otherwise you will reward poor effort by taking the job off their hands.

This is why it is so helpful to devise the standard letters as a team, because this helps to train staff in the art of good letter writing as well as clarifying the messages that you are keen to put across.

Insist that all letters are personally signed — this personal touch really does mean a great deal to the recipient. It also encourages the 'signer' to take more responsibility for their work as they have literally put their name to it.

Faxes

Faxes are most useful when a speedy response is needed and when the 'appearance' of the letter is of less concern. Faxes are particularly useful if you are trying to communicate with customers overseas as they are quicker than airmail and much cheaper.

The drawback of a fax is that its appearance generally depends not only on the quality of your own fax machine, but also the receiving one. Poorly maintained fax equipment can result in your fax arriving in an illegible or 'streaky' condition which is

unattractive and can render its message unreadable.
Also, faxes are not a good way, on the whole, of
transmitting quality pictures, so if you have an
attractive and colourful brochure, it won't fax well.

Some of these issues are changing as technology
improves, but it will take time for organizations and
individuals to update their equipment and so even if
you have the very latest and best equipment, the
recipient may have a very old and fuzzy fax machine
that will output your fax at a very low grade of
appearance.

Some businesses send faxes to ask for confirmation
of telephone orders — making it easy for the customer
just to sign the order and then fax it back. It's quick
and convenient and it catches customers shortly after
they have agreed to purchase so there hasn't been
time for them to change their minds (unlike a
standard letter).

If you are in a hurry, you can write a fax by hand
and for short notes this is perfectly acceptable and
businesslike. But don't write long letters as there are
problems of legibility of handwriting — especially if it
has been faxed.

Reports and proposals

Many of the points relevant to letter writing also
apply to longer documents including reports and
proposals which contain detailed information for the
customer to consider. However, with these types of
documents a clear and well-defined structure is even
more vital. Just as this book is divided into chapters
addressing different subjects, and each chapter is
further subdivided into sections, so any long
document needs to be divided into sections according
to the subject matter.

It is better to plan out the structure of such a document before you begin writing than simply to write down everything you can think of and then try to arrange it into some format. So start with the headings for each section of the document. Ask yourself what the main topics that you want to discuss are. Then try to arrange these into a logical framework.

For example, if you are defining the specifications of a product or service that you want to propose to a customer, then the section headings might include:

- A **summary** giving a brief outline of the whole proposal (picking out what you consider to be the key points). Some people like the summary at the start of the document and others prefer it at the end. As long as it is clearly marked and the reader can easily find it, it doesn't really matter where it is.

- An **introduction** setting out the situation that you propose to change. Many people make the mistake of starting their proposals or reports with information about themselves or their organization, but you need to think about what the reader will be most concerned about and address that issue in the opening paragraphs of your proposals to 'draw them in' to reading the whole document.

- Company **background information** — a short description of the relevant services and track record of your organization.

- **Terms and conditions** — in particular, it's important to inform the customer of any specific requirements (payment within 30 days, payment by direct debit only etc.)

- The **offer** — a clear and succinct description of what you are actually offering whether it is the details of a service or the specifications of a product.

- An **explanation** — a description of how you think your suggestion will help the customer.

- A **justification** — a clear set of reasons why what you propose will work in the way you say it will.

- Any other relevant information — for example, **references** from other happy customers or appropriate comments made by others (e.g. glowing press cuttings).

Clearly you will want to give appropriate headings to these sections and include an index or contents table for longer documents so that it is easy for customers to turn to the appropriate page when they have a specific query. However, your aim will be to order these sections in a way that makes sense and draws the reader into your 'story'. The actual order of these sections may vary greatly from document to document, but it must reflect the likely interest levels of the intended reader if it is to hold their attention.

Summary

Putting things in writing helps to clarify the issues as well as putting them on the record for future reference if necessary. A written document gives the customer time to digest the information and makes it harder for anyone to argue they have been misinformed if the letter is correct and clear.

Standards of written communication can make a big difference to customer perceptions of your organization, so it's important to ensure that letters

are carefully written and even more carefully checked
to ensure they are clear, concise, grammatically
correct, properly spelt and consistent in appearance.
The use of standard letters or even standard
paragraphs inserted as appropriate into individual
letters can ensure both quality and consistency in
your written communications. It can be a very helpful
skill-building exercise to get your staff to work on
creating standard letters for use throughout your
department.

Faxes are a specific form of letter and are most
useful when speed rather than appearance is of the
essence. Faxes are a cost-effective way of contacting
people over long distances and across international
time zones.

All other customer service documentation must
reach the same high standards set for letters, but
longer documents such as reports also need to be well
structured and clearly headed if they are to be read.
At all times, when writing such documents, it is
important to ask: 'What is the reader likely to be
interested in?' and 'How can I make this point more
clearly?' Time spent on redrafting longer documents
may be justified by the greater impact they will have
on customer behaviour.

8
Customer service on the Internet

This chapter looks at one of the fastest growing ways
of communicating with customers: the Internet.
Although the Internet is undoubtedly over-hyped, it
is an important development in communications
technology. It allows companies to reach out and
communicate with customers across the world, 24
hours a day and at a relatively low cost.

Unlike many of the traditional forms of customer
contact (brochures, letters, flyers and telephone calls)
the Internet costs pretty much the same whether one
person or one million people access a web site. The
majority of the cost lies in setting up and maintaining
a web site, and servicing any enquiries that result.

A well-designed, informative and easy-to-use web
site should reduce the number of additional enquiries
that customers need to make, whilst increasing the
number of orders that they place. However, you do
need to inform all your customers of your web
address and make sure it is registered with the
popular Internet search engines.

Who is on the Internet?

The first point to make clear is that it is not just people in anoraks — an increasing number of 'ordinary' people access the Internet whether from home or from work. Recent estimates (by market research firm BMRB) put the number of connections as high as 3.4 million in the UK alone. The BRMB report also indicates a movement towards the mass consumer market with increased take-up by women and non-professionals. This report predicts a take-up rate of 40 per cent for the UK by the year 2000. However, other surveys of Internet use suggest that it is still strongly dominated by young, professional men: a Henley Management Institute report suggests that 71 per cent of net users are men and that 62 per cent of them are below the age of 35. Nearly half are from the AB class.

According to a 1997 DTI report, one in four British companies is connected to the Internet and one in six has a web site, so this is not an issue that managers can afford to ignore.

Market penetration varies from sector to sector. The 'youth market' is particularly well served with most colleges and all universities being able to offer access to their students. Home computing is a popular activity and 28 per cent of homes in the UK boast a PC. Connection to the Internet is a relatively low cost item — it is a very competitive marketplace for the Internet Service Providers which enable individuals and organizations to link up to the World Wide Web.

Clearly there are many customers — both business and personal — who have access to the Internet, which explains why it is a significant issue for any manager with customer service responsibilities. This number is growing at the rate of 12 per cent per year. This is likely to increase even more rapidly as information supply companies like Teletext and

Phillips compete to make it easier and easier to connect to the Internet — by the use of television set-top boxes rather than by traditional computers.

Web sites — what can they do for you and your customers?

A web site is a set of pages of information which can include text, pictures, sound, video and animations although there are some technical issues that can restrict the quality and value of each of these items. The pages of a site are connected together and to the rest of the World Wide Web by 'links' that allow the user to 'jump' from page to page simply by clicking on special areas of the page (often these take the form of on-screen buttons or underlined words or phrases).

Because users can 'hop about' it is easy for them to get lost and to miss useful information which is why it is absolutely vital that web sites are well designed and carefully structured. It must be obvious at a glance how customers can find out the information they need, make further enquiries or place their orders. You don't want to lose your customer until they have explored your site and made contact if appropriate.

Exploring a badly designed web site can be a bit like playing a game of snakes and ladders where you can slip through trapdoors and shoot up ladders to new pages without any real sense of the overall picture. It is irritating to the user and can result in a speedy departure from the site — never to return.

Your company's web site

There are lots of design and technical issues related to web sites, but the most important point is that your site is *usable* and *customer friendly*. Even if the web site is controlled by a completely different department, you should go and try it for yourself. If you get lost, confused or irritated then the chances are that your customers will be feeling the same way and you should give this feedback to the relevant person in your organization.

Tesco web site: a useful example

The web site put up by the supermarket chain, Tesco, is a good example of how Internet technology can be used to communicate with customers. The site offers customers a number of possibilities:

- on-line shopping for mail order items like wine, perfume and flowers

- on-line shopping for groceries to be delivered to customers in selected areas of the country (Tesco is testing the idea out)

- answers to frequently asked questions (FAQs) — although these mostly concentrate on Internet-related issues rather than being of general interest

- recipes

- downloadable software for wine selection

- an illustrated description of its customer care policies

- the opportunity for customers to comment, using email

The site is not complex, and it is therefore relatively easy to navigate around. It uses encryption for its on-line ordering services which means that not all its customers will be able to use these services (some encryption security is not compatible with some browsers), but this does mean that customers should feel secure when giving their credit card details over the Internet. Tesco also offers to get a telesales person to phone customers to take credit card details after they've placed their order on-line if customers are nervous of giving these details over the Internet.
You can visit this site at the following address:

http://www.tesco.co.uk

This shows the benefit of a nice simple and obvious address — it's easy for customers to 'guess'.

Some services you can offer on a web site include:

- Updates on the latest goods or services your organization has to offer.

- Technical information and up-to-date specifications.

- Pictures of goods/services and text describing and promoting your organization.

- FAQs (frequently asked questions and their answers) as an information service.

- 'Resources' — information that your customers might find useful or relevant.

- Links to other sites which are relevant to your customers (reciprocal links can encourage more people to visit your site).

- Email links to relevant staff or to the 'customer service department' so that you make it easy for customers to make enquiries and give feedback.

- Interactive forms for customers to fill in on-line to order goods, request more information etc.

Online ideas

Some examples of ideas for customer service pages on the web are available at a site the authors have specially created to accompany this book, which can be found at:

http://www.ful.co.uk/cusbk.html

If your company doesn't currently have a web site...

The only reason to have a site is if your organization thinks that some of the people it needs to communicate with are Internet users. Even though maintaining a site is relatively inexpensive, it can be costly to set one up as it may be necessary to employ the services of a specialist web design company. So it's important to ask the following questions:

- Do a significant number of our customers use the Internet?

- Does Internet use impact buying decisions?

- What message do we want to communicate via the Internet? (It is a particularly useful technology to support frequent updates of information about products/services.)

- Are our competitors on the Internet? And if so, what messages are they communicating or what services are they offering?

Like any form of promotion or communication with customers, you must be able to justify the costs of a web site in business terms. Businesses with web sites are usually very coy about how much business they actually do over the Internet, and tend to talk about it in terms of 'this is where the future lies' rather than 'this is good business today'. However, it is true that in a fast-moving marketplace, it is unwise to wait until you have been left behind to start running.

One useful immediate action is to browse the Internet yourself. Look up your competitors and test out their sites. Some libraries and cafés offer cheap access to the Internet and are a good place to start. Ask friends/colleagues for recommendations of good sites to visit. Use the Internet to find information about a hobby or pastime — and in this way you will get a feel for what makes a site useful and interesting. Then if your organization decides to take the plunge, you will be prepared to offer useful ideas and perhaps participate in setting it up.

You could consider initiating the project yourself: a well-designed and carefully thought-out web site is a useful customer service point if your customers are able to access it. They can look at it at any time of the day or night. A 1997 survey found that while very few people actually made purchases over the Internet, many used it to gather information to support their buying decisions. According to research carried out by The Internet Research Company, successful web sites were those that complemented and reinforced brand positions created and presented by other forms of sales promotion.

In particular, customers respond best to detailed, constantly updated information and the chance to interact with the company. So if you are considering proposing a web site, it is important to remember to allocate resources for updating and maintaining the 'currency' of the information it contains. It is essential to make arrangements for the site to be regularly 'refreshed' with new and relevant items, so that people have a reason to return to it regularly.

Email

Email (electronic mail — the process of communicating via computer networks) is a very popular use of the Internet as it allows information to be passed around the world very quickly and at a very low cost. More than 40 per cent of British businesses said they used email, according to a 1997 DTI survey.

Email systems are usually easy to use provided you know the exact address of the person to whom you want to send a message. This ease of use plus the benefits of speedy and cheap communication have fuelled the growth of email use over the past decade.

Email originated in the academic community simply because the universities and research institutes were the first groups of organizations to network their computer systems. This resulted in a very casual messaging style — email was more akin to 'chatting' than to formal letters. Some of that informality carries over today even though the Internet connects a greater variety of individuals, businesses and other organizations (including governmental agencies).

This informality is not just an accident of history, but also a consequence of the nature of email — because messages can be sent and received very quickly, it is more like phoning than writing in some respects. It is also feasible to send very brief messages of a single line — unburdened by the conventions of formal letter writing. This makes it quick to read and much quicker to write.

Managers tend to have their own email access — the messages arrive on the personal computers on their desktops. As a result, they are far less likely to ask a secretary to read through incoming or type outgoing email messages which makes them more direct and personal. Managers tend to keep messages short, so they don't have to spend a long time typing.

One of the interesting aspects of email is that because the information is received in an electronic format, you are able to edit the messages that you receive. This, in turn, means that you can simply annotate a message and send it back.

It might be considered rude to scribble on a customer's letter and post it back, but it is perfectly polite to copy a customer's emailed enquiry and type in your response to each point and then send it back as your reply. It shows that you have dealt with the enquiry personally and individually, rather than sending back a standard response. This has the added benefit in the way that it tends to ensure that you deal with the customer's enquiry fully.

Some of the advantages and disadvantages that email offers to businesses are given in the table below.

Advantages	Disadvantages
Cheap to send messages — it can cost no more than a local phone call to send as many messages as you have prepared at any one time. It costs even less if you're emailing a colleague in the same organization	Cost of installing email system and maintaining it adds to existing communications costs
International emails cost no more than local messages	Can cut down 'personal' contact with customers in favour of communicating from the desktop which may eventually ruin customer relationships
Its informal and direct nature makes for better communication	Can encourage laziness and sloppiness in communication as a result
Casual format can make for friendlier communications — even between people who have never met each other	Casual format can lead to carelessness and unintended insult
Can send documents/messages to a long list of people at the click of a single button once an email list has been set up	Can result in desktop computers being clogged with lots of irrelevant email messages
Can copy messages and documents straight on to computer hard disk and edit in a word processing package which makes co-authoring documents easier	Can lose/delete messages by mistake or by computer error
Easy to keep in touch with a wide range of business contacts (including suppliers and customers) by sending occasional email messages	Can waste hours writing email messages that don't meet any real business objective
Quick to send and only short delay before it's received	But depends on the other person accessing their email system to pick up messages — if they don't check incoming mail regularly the advantage of speed can be lost
Allows staff to batch responses to customer enquiries and thus makes work more efficient	Can mean staff put off responding to customer enquiries and customers go elsewhere

Management issues

There are some general management issues to be aware of in relation to use of both the Internet and email. As has been mentioned earlier, email tends to be a fairly casual method of communicating, and it's important to remind staff that agreements entered into via email are just as binding as formal written contracts. For this reason, employees should keep copies of their non-trivial email correspondence.

Some email systems automatically keep copies of every message sent or received. This can be useful, but if you have a lot of message traffic, it can also lead to disks becoming full of non-essential messages. This is especially true if staff are on email group lists which send out lots of mail, and if email is used to send substantial documents electronically. The ability to 'attach' documents created in other software packages to email messages is useful, but can lead to large volumes of data being transferred unnecessarily. Some email systems limit the size of files that can be transferred in this way.

You may find it easier to keep print-outs in traditional files rather than storing all the messages on disk where they can easily be inadvertently deleted or amended. Also, by keeping email print-outs in files with regular correspondence, it is easier for someone picking up a file to find out the full picture of any communications with a customer rather than only a partial picture. And you will be able to occasionally audit email messages to ensure that they conform with your organization's policies and practices.

Employees can use email for personal communications — as many of their friends will have email addresses at work also. This may have the benefit of cutting down personal phone calls in some instances, but is harder to monitor. It is important to set clear boundaries for personal use of work facilities and make sure that every member of staff understands them.

However, it is also important to remember that 'play' is an important part of the learning process — if you don't allow staff some latitude to explore the facilities on offer (perhaps motivated by personal interests) then you will restrict the speed of skill acquisition. For example, a person with a passion for hot air balloons may spend some time investigating relevant sites on the World Wide Web. Although this is not relevant to his or her job, he or she may acquire useful Internet search strategies and discover valuable shortcuts as well as becoming more familiar with the Internet environment as a whole.

It is always a balance between encouraging people to explore the facilities on offer and tightly focusing their activities and energy on the objectives of the organization. The balance you reach depends on your need for the skills concerned and the pressures of your day-to-day work. It may be possible to encourage people to learn by allowing them to pursue their personal interests, using your organization's facilities out of working hours. In this way you may encourage staff to acquire potentially valuable skills that will benefit both the individuals concerned and the organization as a whole.

Summary

The Internet is a useful way of communicating with customers who have on-line access. It is a growth area of communications, and even if you feel that your existing customer base does not have access to it, you need to be aware of developments in this area as more and more people get connected.

Web sites can act as useful customer service points if they are easy to find and use.

A good web site provides your customers and prospective customers with relevant and up-to-date information on the subjects they are likely to be interested in. Our experience of both using and building web sites suggests that it is very important to plan your web site before you begin to implement it. There are limitations to the sort of information that you are able to offer over the Internet, but it is ideal for conveying text and simple graphics.

Email is a cheap and convenient form of communication that is very popular with the people who have ready access to it. It can be used to respond to customer enquiries in a personal, friendly and immediate way. However, email can be very time-consuming because it is so easy to send lots of messages.

Further ideas can be accessed at:
http://www.ful/cusbk.html

9
Complaint handling — resolving problems and empathizing with customers

In today's competitive market, customer retention is vital to business success — it is usually easier and less costly to maintain and develop existing accounts than it is to recruit new ones. Handling customer complaints effectively not only resolves immediate problems but is also an excellent way of building customer satisfaction and gaining customer loyalty.

When customers complain, they are giving an organization the chance to put things right. Research shows than less than 10 per cent of customers ever communicate with companies, whether they offer good or bad service. Of those with complaints only a small percentage bother to contact customer relations: these usually turn out to be the most loyal customers if their problems are dealt with efficiently.

Just as staff can improve performance by listening to constructive criticism and adjusting their behaviour appropriately, so organizations can become more profitable by listening to the needs and problems of their customers. Complaints provide valuable feedback in a number of ways:

- they show what is important to the customer
- they lead to improvements that are customer focused
- they supplement market information
- well-handled, they bind the customer to the organization and its product more closely than before.

Building customer loyalty

Changing wants, needs and expectations means that it is essential to evaluate customer satisfaction on an ongoing basis. Loyal customers who find an organization's product and its customer service staff responsive to their unique needs not only remain loyal to the company but often act as an excellent public relations device, spreading the good word and so recruiting new customers.

Maintaining customer loyalty includes recovering when something goes wrong as well as providing an excellent service when things are going right.

In fact, research shows that if a company excels in the recovery process when mistakes happen, customers' faith in the company is not just restored, it is often strengthened. If customer complaints are ignored then not only are customers likely to go elsewhere but they may also deter other potential customers with damaging accounts of their experiences.

A company seldom has a chance to build up such loyalty unless customers come forward in the first place. For this reason alone, it more than pays to provide customers with numerous opportunities to express their dissatisfaction. This includes:

- asking customers if they are satisfied

- providing freephone customer comment numbers

- fully involving front-line employees in the crusade to identify and help customers frustrated by service or product failures

- regular questionnaires designed to gauge customer satisfaction

- regularly reviewing approaches to dealing with customer problems.

Quick and accurate responses to customer problems and an active approach to customer needs — approaching customers to find out what they think rather than waiting for problems to arise — helps to forestall potential concerns and put them right before customers defect. This process can take a small amount of effort but produce great long-term results

Not all defectors should be retained however. The unreasonable demands of unhappy customers whose needs do not fit with the company's capabilities can devour excessive resources and wreak havoc on employee morale. Identifying these customers is an important managerial task which calls for analysis of both customer profitability and consideration of the company's core activities. 'Difficult' customers who buy goods/services that are peripheral or not particularly profitable to your organization may be more trouble that they are worth.

ːwing complaints as opportunities

ːnning customer loyalty through efficient complaint
ːndling depends to a great extent on the
organization's approach towards complaints.
Complaints should be welcomed as an opportunity to
improve customer relations and used as a means to
find out how products and services can be adapted to
meet changing customer needs. When this happens
more customers are likely to achieve long-term
satisfaction, ensuring the continued profitability of the
organization.

However, as most people will have experienced,
many companies take on a 'defensive' approach to
complaints which serves to alienate customers. An
unhappy customer is likely to actively seek an
alternative supplier and is an easy target for
competitors.

Debating whether the customer is correctly
perceiving the facts is a non-starter if the goal is to
retain customer business:

- If the company replies to a customer and claims
  that events did not happen as the customer
  suggested then the customer perceives the
  company to be calling him or her a liar.

- If, after investigating, the company reports back to
  the customer that events indeed took place as the
  customer claimed, then the customer may become
  even more agitated because he or she will infer
  that the company did not believe him or her at
  first.

- If the company relays information to the customer
  that he or she did not know, the customer may
  think that the company is trying to make excuses
  for poor service.

Think about your experiences with some of your
suppliers — how many times have you heard excuses
like: 'It's got nothing to do with me, the accounts
department must have got it wrong,' 'You'll have to
ring back as the person you need to speak to isn't
available at the moment,' 'We haven't got any record
of it, you must have made a mistake.'

Think how you feel when somebody perhaps
blocks you, implies that it's your fault or blames a
colleague. Now put yourself in your customers'
shoes. How does your organization treat them when
they want to complain?

One of the biggest obstacles to productive
complaint handling is the feeling of *guilt* which
complaints can so easily generate. Staff waste time
and energy trying to defend themselves by trying to
shift the blame. This does not help solve the
customer's problem but it does serve to aggravate the
situation further.

Chris Argyris, a Harvard Business School
professor, suggests that many of us tend to have very
defensive approaches when faced with stress. He
suggests that our behaviour is driven by the need to
stay in control, avoid embarrassment, risk or
appearance of incompetence. These are negative
motivators and don't lead to an openness to change
and improvement — especially when dealing with
customers.

What makes the problem worse is that many
organizations conspire with their employees to create
organizationally defensive routines that mimic the
ones that we have learnt as individuals. Instead of
facing up to a mistake and taking action to correct it,
many organizations indulge in bouts of 'face-saving'
and 'sweeping under the carpet'. People are
encouraged to rationalize their failures and to lay the

blame elsewhere in the organization or outside if possible.

A major challenge in managing complaint handling is for the organization — from the top down — to adopt a positive approach to complaints so that they are seen as opportunities for the organization to grow and not as attacks that must be fought off. This ensures that individuals feel that they will be supported by management in any recovery actions that they take, which makes it more likely that they will deal with problems effectively rather than hide them to avoid getting into trouble.

Employees won't always make the right moves but it is better that they make occasional mistakes rather than not trying to solve customers' problems because of fear of the consequences. Managers need to avoid coming down like 'a ton of bricks' on a member of staff who makes a wrong decision. Instead, it is better to explain why the decision was incorrect and what a more appropriate action would have been. Then, the next time the individual is confronted with a similar situation, he or she will be better equipped to deal with it.

Communicating with customers

Once an organization develops a positive attitude towards complaints, the next step is to ensure that staff are capable of responding to what they understand customers' complaints to be.

People on the front line ultimately create value since they are the ones who determine the kinds of experience that the organization generates for its customers and poor communication is cited as one of the major causes of mistakes.

Good communication should ensure a two
understanding of the situation between staff and
customers. If customers feel that they have suffered
the hands of the organization, situations can become
emotionally charged, causing a communication
breakdown. In this case, it is even more important for
customer service representatives to remain in control
of their own emotions, articulate well and, probably
most important of all, *listen* to what customers have to
say (see table at end of this chapter for tips).

Developing strong recovery processes

Another essential element in successful complaint
handling is an efficient recovery process. Most
customers can understand that mistakes sometimes
happen but if they do, they want them put right
quickly. Front-line customer service staff can make an
excellent job of dealing with dissatisfied customers
but if strong back-up processes are unavailable then
they are fighting a losing battle. Morale is seriously
damaged if staff find that they cannot live up to their
promises.

Strong recovery processes depend on excellent
interdepartmental communication and co-operation.
If corrective action is subjugated to 'finger pointing'
and 'blame allocating' then problems become worse
and organizations enter into a downward spiral of
increasingly poor customer service and
dissatisfaction.

Working through errors is a test of internal co-
operation and requires each department to take
responsibility for their particular link in the customer
satisfaction chain as well as a commitment to open
and honest communication with the aim of improving

customer service. For example, if the wrong order has been sent to the customer it is important to:

- identify the problem and correct the error
- identify the cause of the error
- decide on the action that needs to be taken to prevent the error from being repeated.

Each department that has handled the order needs to get involved with the solution to the problem, to prevent it from recurring. The solution can only be achieved through co-operation and communication between departments. This means that every person has to consider themselves part of a company-wide team working towards giving customers a quality service. The strength of team commitment will be measured when your team comes up against another department's errors and can continue to develop a better working relationship after corrective action has been taken.

Successful complaint handling is more than sticking plaster on a problem, it is the ability to prevent it from happening again. Managers can aid prevention by making sure that the lines of communication are kept open. This could entail regular departmental meetings with the aim of keeping every employee abreast of current problems and important developments.

Ensuring that front-line staff have a broad knowledge of what is happening behind the scenes makes it easier for them to be effective. For example, if the production team knows that certain products are going to take a week longer to be manufactured than originally planned then they need to pass this detailed information on to the service staff. The service department can then give customers exact information on delivery dates rather than annoying them with vague estimates or excuses. Similarly, if the service department is receiving a large amount of complaints about a particular product then this information should be passed on to the appropriate department so that the root of the problem which may rest in its original design can be dealt with.

Complaint handling techniques

Specific training on how your organization deals with complaints is essential to provide staff with the support and knowledge that they need to deal with the wide variety of complaints that can arise. However, there are several steps that can make complaint handling more successful whatever the situation:

Listening to gain an objective overview
Full concentration should be given to the customer's story so that staff act on facts and not assumptions. Debating whether the customer has perceived the situation correctly is not of immediate concern. To hold on to customers, service staff need to deal with perceptions even if they are totally inaccurate. Paraphrasing and repeating back what customers have said is an excellent way to check understanding and to convince the customer that they really are being listened to.

It's sometimes difficult to remain objective in emotionally charged situations but it is necessary to *remain calm and open-minded* to get to the bottom of the problem. Allowing the customer to tell their story without interruption often serves to calm the customer down as well as giving an insight into what has gone wrong. It is particularly important to avoid 'negative' listening or incorrect assumptions.

Empathizing with the customer

It is important that staff show that they understand how customers feel. This doesn't necessarily mean that they agree with these feelings or the customer's point of view — customers are likely to get things wrong too. But empathizing with customers shows them that they are being listened to and that somebody is willing to help them. If customers feel the attention they receive is genuinely caring and tailored to meet their needs, it is far more likely that they will develop trust and confidence in the organization.

Apologizing and 'owning' the problem

Customers become irritated and disillusioned with organizations who make it difficult for them to complain. Whoever receives the complaint should take responsibility for putting things right — that is, if they can't handle it, they should contact a colleague who can solve the problem and put them in contact with the customer rather than making the customer do the leg work.

Customers don't generally want to know who made the mistake but they do want to be assured that things can be put right promptly. When a customer complains it's essential that the customer service representative dealing with him or her apologizes for what has happened and makes a commitment to put things right even if this only includes putting the person in contact with a colleague who is better able to help them.

Customers should always be treated with respect and consideration. Resolving problems not only gives an organization a chance to show how responsive it is but can also be an excellent opportunity to find out more about the customer's needs and expectations. This information can be used to interest them in other products and services that are available.

Taking action to resolve the complaint
The complaint should be investigated and resolved promptly. When complaints cannot be dealt with immediately many companies set themselves deadlines, for example a resolution time of 24 hours.

If more time is needed to accommodate the customer, he or she should be kept informed and given a time when they can expect further information or a solution. Some organizations have found that customers with problems are delighted to be telephoned by a member of the customer service team. A 'personal' service shows the customer that they are valued by the company.

If too long a time is taken to solve problems, it's likely that the customers won't wait around but will move to a competitor. A speedy reply demonstrates a sense of urgency; it shows that the company really cares about the customer's feelings and situation. Customers are more likely to remain loyal if they are confident that the operational problem that they encountered will truly be addressed.

Follow up the complaint to ensure satisfaction
The complainer needs to be contacted with an explanation, offer of compensation, description of how the problem will be corrected or a rejection of the complaint — whatever is appropriate. It's a good idea to follow up with written correspondence to confirm what has been agreed and to apologize for any inconvenience.

Positive listening	Negative listening
Diagnostic: remain non-judgemental as any comments or criticism will inhibit customer's flow. Keep own emotions in check and show interest through eye-contact and words of encouragement like: 'Go on...' and 'I understand so far...'. Assist discovery of whole story from customer's point of view.	**Distracted:** occurs when two tasks are done simultaneously — common when using phone. Instead of stopping and paying attention to what the customer says, an opinion is formed on the basis of a partially attended exchange. Leads to misunderstandings and mistakes.
Empathetic: put yourself in customer's shoes. Viewing complaints from their point of view makes it easier to appreciate the problem. Can diffuse emotional situations as customers realize that you are willing to listen to what they're saying. Use phrases like: 'I can understand how you feel...' and 'That must have been very annoying for you...'.	**Dismissive:** you've already made up your mind about what the customer is trying to say or attend only to information that confirms or supports your immediate opinion. Leads to formation of inaccurate opinions or ideas on the situation.
Reflective: paraphrase and repeat back to confirm understanding of what has been said. Prevents errors and mistakes. Also, when idea is repeated back to customer he or she may become aware of its true implications and perhaps realize that they have made a mistake.	**Judgemental:** involves passing judgement before much, if anything, is said — often based on first impressions such as appearance and accent. Easy to obtain the wrong idea and guaranteed to infuriate customers.
Neutral: look to find out the facts of the situation not to lay or avoid blame. Neutral approach allows whole complaint to be heard and attended to without getting over-emotional or defensive.	**Emotional:** become perhaps aggressive or defensive. May be blinded by emotions and lose ability to get the facts straight and sort out the problem properly. Emotional response may also provoke emotional behaviour from customer.

Summary

Most people understand that mistakes sometimes happen. If their problems are resolved quickly and easily they are usually very reasonable and may develop a greater loyalty to the company.

It is cheaper and easier to maintain existing customers than to seek new ones, it makes sense to develop a complaint handling process that convinces the customer that your company is competent, professional and worth dealing with in the long term:

- Only 5 per cent of customers bother to complain.

- Research shows that dealing with complaints successfully increases customer loyalty.

- Complaints provide valuable feedback on how the company can become more successful.

- The best approach to complaints, from the top of the organization down, is to see them as opportunities to improve customer relations. A defensive attitude that appears to pass the blame aggravates the situation further and encourages customers to defect.

- It's better for employees to make mistakes than not to try to solve the customer's problem because they fear that they'll get into trouble.

- Excellent communication skills are a major key to successful complaint handling.

- Strong recovery processes are needed to help staff resolve complaints. This often requires inter-departmental communication and co-operation.

- The process for complaint handling should include listening, empathizing, apologizing, owning the problem, taking action and following up.

10
Dealing with angry customers

For most customer service staff, angry customers are unusual. The fewer angry customers that staff meet the better, but also the less prepared they may be to handle such an encounter. The exception to this may be found in some governmental agencies where staff regularly have to deal with angry or emotionally overwrought clients. People who have been evicted from their homes or have not received their social security cheques are more likely to be hostile and aggressive than people who have bought a piece of faulty garden furniture. Of course, this is not always the case — if the faulty garden furniture resulted in an elderly mother falling on to the patio and breaking her hip, then emotions may well run high.

Staff working for the social services are often specially trained to handle 'hostile clients', but this sort of training is less likely to be offered to a customer assistant in a furniture store. However, it is important to prepare all customer service staff to deal with aggressive customers because although they may be few in number they can have a disproportionately negative effect — and if they are badly handled the situation can escalate rapidly out of control. Verbal aggression can quickly turn into physical aggression in some instances, so it is vital to understand how to prevent this happening if at all possible.

As a manager you need to be prepared to handle all sorts of 'angry encounters' — with staff as well as with customers. If a customer does appear very upset, your staff may well call on you to deal with the problem, figuring that you have the authority and the experience to handle the situation, so you must be prepared.

There are three key elements to dealing with a difficult customer that you personally control:

- **Attitude** — how you feel about the situation.

- **Behaviour** — how you act in the situation (not necessarily reflecting how you feel).

- **Knowledge** — of what you can do within your organization's constraints.

This chapter looks at each of these in a little more detail and then goes on to consider what you should do when approached by an angry customer.

Attitude

How do you feel if one of your staff asks you to deal with 'Mr Jones' who is very angry about something your organization has done? Do you feel tense? Does your stomach churn? Do your palms start to sweat? What goes through your mind as you approach Mr Jones? Have you already started to prepare your excuses, to justify your organization's actions? Have you formed a judgement of Mr Jones on the basis of his appearance?

All these reactions are perfectly natural, but mostly unhelpful, so you need to learn to identify your immediate emotional response to this kind of problem and separate yourself from it. And the way to do this is to remember that, in most circumstances, the person is not angry with you personally (even if he or she is very personal in his or her attack), but angry with what you represent. In such situations it is very helpful to see yourself as distinct from your job. The angry customer is shouting at your 'job' not at you — even though you're the one standing there listening to it. This distinction is absolutely crucial if you are to keep your own emotions in check.

If you take the customer's anger personally you will feel bad about the situation and be less able to handle it calmly, so you will damage yourself as well as the relationship with the customer. You will find it harder not to take things personally if you have played some part in provoking the situation, perhaps by displaying inefficiency or an unhelpful attitude.

It is not always easy to make a distinction between yourself and your job, but unless you try to do this, you will find it very hard to resolve angry encounters satisfactorily. You may not be able to suppress all your emotions, but you can certainly choose the ways in which you express them.

If you start to feel your temper fraying, then think about the following points:

- This person is saying these things to me because I represent my organization, they don't know me at all and are not addressing me personally.

- I am a manager and my job is to manage the situation — not get caught up in it.

- This person is very upset and needs to shout at someone — I can handle that.

- I want to resolve this situation so I need to think about the issues not the emotions.

- I will not take any of these comments personally because they relate to my job.

Prejudices

Be aware of your own prejudices. We all have them, but if you're aware of them you can prevent them from controlling your actions. There is a common tendency to judge people on their appearances, the way they speak or even the clothes they wear: common but unhelpful.

There are practical considerations as well as ethical reasons for not jumping to conclusions based on first impressions — you can be totally wrong and put yourself at a real disadvantage if you make a false assumption simply based on appearance or according to stereotype.

Awareness of a prejudice is the first step towards overcoming it. It is better to make yourself aware of your own prejudices in private while you're feeling calm than to have them exposed in front of customers or staff in a tense atmosphere. Try taking a piece of paper and writing down any strong opinions about 'groups of people' that you hold ('groups' can include ethnic groups, income groups or even political groups). You are not going to show this piece of paper to anyone else, so be as honest as you can. This is quite a difficult exercise as most of us like to think we are fair-minded and shy away from confronting our own prejudices.

Once you have managed to write down some negative attitudes about other people, examine them carefully — question your assumptions and challenge your own attitudes. Do you have real grounds for the opinions you hold or are they views that you have picked up from others? Do you think that all individuals belonging to the group you have specified would behave in the same way? Are you a member of a 'group' and do you share all your characteristics with that group? At the end of this exercise tear up your sheet of paper and throw it away — and try to let go of some of your prejudices at the same time.

Remember that every member of a group is an individual in his or her own right and will not necessarily fit your stereotype.

However, if you spend all your time thinking about how you feel, you won't listen properly to the customer and this will reduce your chances of finding a successful resolution. So you need to focus on the *content* of what the customer is saying rather than the *way* it is said and block out any personal abuse.

Finally, it is useful if you can take a positive approach to the problems raised by hostile customers. So that instead of thinking: 'Oh no, I don't want to deal with this,' you manage to see it more as a challenge to your professional skills: 'What's the best way to handle this?' You need to go into the situation looking for a solution rather than an argument. Your aim is to work with the customer and negotiate a satisfactory outcome that is acceptable to you both.

Behaviour

Perhaps one of the most important parts of dealing with an angry customer is to ensure that you don't behave in such a way as to provoke an outburst of aggression. For this reason, it's important to adopt open, positive and non-aggressive body language. This is easier to say than do. Unconsciously we express our feelings in our posture and gestures. It is easier to lie with words than it is with your body language. That's why it's important to address your underlying attitude rather than simply follow a list of behavioural instructions. If you are feeling confident about handling a situation and not feeling personally threatened, insecure or angry, then you have a much greater chance of behaving in a non-confrontational way.

However, even if you are feeling anxious or irritated, don't allow your posture or gestures to communicate these feelings to the other person.

Don't

✗ Fold your arms tightly against your chest (defensive)

✗ Point with your fingers (aggressive)

✗ Lean forward or stand over the customer (aggressive)

✗ Get too close to the customer (invading their 'personal space' is aggressive)

✗ Turn away from the customer (disinterested)

✗ Stare fixedly at the customer (aggressive)

✗ Gesture with any implement (e.g. a pencil, ruler or any other item as this is aggressive)

✗ Hunch your shoulders (defensive)

✗ Back away from the customer (defensive and can show that the customer is successfully intimidating you)

✗ Touch the customer (unless it is to shake hands, but only do this if the person is not overly aggressive or you have concluded an agreement)

Do

✓ Stand in an open relaxed posture or sit if the customer is sitting down

✓ Hold your hands, palms outward, loosely by your sides

✓ Make eye contact regularly to show you are listening

✓ Nod your head to show you understand and are listening to the points that the customer is making

✓ Smile on greeting the customer (but not when they're telling you why they're angry)

✓ Look confident that you can sort out the situation (if your hands are shaking badly, hide them in your pockets as it's better to look a bit casual than to look terrified)

✓ Make 'open' gestures with your hands

Your aim is to present a confident, but open demeanour so that the customer is not threatened by you, but does not get the impression either that you can be bullied or intimidated.

Your personal safety and that of your staff is paramount — it's important to minimize risks, but this can be a difficult decision. For example, if a customer appears on the edge of violence, then naturally you don't want to be left alone with that person. On the other hand, trying to deal with this customer with a couple of other members of staff acting as your 'bodyguards' can look intimidating and can trigger the violence you want to prevent. It is usually better to deal with angry customers in private, but not if it looks like they might attack you. You have to use your judgement based on the factors in front of you.

Violence is a far less likely outcome if you approach customers in a way that makes them feel like you are going to listen to them. The vast majority of angry customers are angry because they feel frustrated and ignored — they feel that they have been let down by your organization and that nobody cares. It may be that their expectations are unreasonable or that they are 'making a mountain out of a molehill' but you have to deal with their perceptions first before you can get into a reasonable discussion of what you can do to sort things out.

Empathy is defined as 'the power of *understanding* and imaginatively entering into another person's feelings' and is different from sympathy which means *sharing* another person's feelings. This difference is critical: you can empathize with a customer without necessarily agreeing with them. Useful empathy-building phrases include:

- 'I can see that you are very upset about what's happened, would you like to tell me the details?'

- 'I can understand that it must be very frustrating for you, perhaps I can help to sort things out...'

- 'I can appreciate that you feel angry about this issue, but I can only help if you talk me through it step by step.'

The aim is to show the customer that you understand their feelings and that you want to help to resolve matters. Encouraging the customer to explain the problem can often go a long way towards making the customer feel better.

Knowledge

For you to be effective in resolving the problems of upset customers you need to know your own organization's policies and the limits of your authority. You also need to understand your organization's processes and procedures so that you can evaluate the customer's complaint in terms of how likely it is and why the situation may have occurred.

If the customer appears out of the blue, then you won't have had a chance to do any investigation, but if the customer arrives by appointment, then it is your responsibility to check the files and gather any relevant evidence before you speak to him or her so that you stand a better chance of resolving matters there and then.

If you don't know your facts (whether they relate to the individual scenario or to your organization's procedures) you will feel uncertain of your ground and this insecurity will communicate to the customer just at the time when you need to be feeling totally confident. This is why it is vital to be completely at ease with your company's policies and procedures: you must know what you're talking about.

What do you do?

Assuming that you have a positive attitude, you are practised in appearing assertive but non-confrontational and you know your company's policies backwards, what do you actually *do* when confronted by an angry customer?

Take control of the situation

- Relax: breathe deeply and make sure that you are feeling calm and in control.

- Greet the customer pleasantly and introduce yourself clearly: 'Hello Mr Smith, my name is Jill Harding and I'm the customer services manager. I am sorry to hear there has been a problem with your account, but I am here to sort matters out.'

- Invite the customer to move to a more private area, as it's best to deal with anger in a quiet and calm environment. Arguments in a public area also give other customers a bad impression of your organization. But if you think there's a possibility of violence, don't go into a room alone with them. Some people enjoy the attention they get from a scene in a public place and will be unwilling to move, don't try to force them to move as you may provoke them further.

Find out what the real problem is...

- Ask the customer to talk you through the difficulty (use a non-personal expression like 'the difficulty' rather than saying something like: 'Tell me about *your* problem,' as that sounds like you have already decided it's not your fault).

- Listen attentively, showing empathy and sincere concern. Often the act of listening will dissipate some of the customer's anger. Try to get a sense of what has really upset the customer rather than just the facts of the matter — what is the real key to the issue: is it disappointment, frustration or irritation? Do they sound like they want restitution, compensation or perhaps a sincere apology?

- Express empathy for their situation and show personal concern to sort the matter out.

- Use very open questions to help the customer express his or her anger. Reflective questions can be particularly helpful if someone is very upset — simply pick out what seems to be the key word in a complaint and restate it as a question: 'You say you were very *disappointed* in our service?'

- Do not interrogate the customer — ask questions carefully and non-judgementally.

- Thank the customer for drawing the matter to your attention and apologize once again for the upset that they have felt. You are not necessarily accepting that they are right but you are acknowledging their distress.

- Once people have calmed down because they feel you are listening to them and they have had a chance to express their emotions, you can move on to the facts of the matter. Try to get a clear sense of *what* happened *when*, as people do tend to exaggerate circumstances or create stories that put their actions in the best possible light and your organization's in the worst possible light. They may hark back to some long-gone incident and make it sound like yesterday, so it's important to check out when events took place as well as what occurred.

Look for solutions

- Use your judgement — can you resolve this problem here and now or will you have to investigate it further? Sometimes people just want an apology and a promise of better service in the future. Other times you will have to check the evidence of your own customer files if you are going to compensate the customer. Perhaps you can agree a solution — you promise to deliver a replacement within 24 hours. Or perhaps the matter is rather more serious and will require senior management intervention (complaints of fraud or false accounting, for example).

- Agree a course of action with the customer — tell them what you propose to do about the matter and ask if that will satisfy them. If you need to investigate matters further promise that you will contact them as soon as you have sorted out what's happened and that you will definitely have an answer for them on a given date. Don't be vague about any follow-up actions — give precise details of what you intend to do. Ask if your course of action is acceptable — try to get an agreement from the customer that your proposals are satisfactory.

- If the customer is wrong, be prepared to say so as tactfully as possible — don't give in, but don't provoke further argument if you can help it. Stick to an outline of the facts and express your belief that there has been a 'misunderstanding'. Try to find a 'face-saver' for the customer — perhaps you can acknowledge that your organization's terms and conditions are badly expressed and then you can thank the customer for pointing this problem out and say that you will suggest improvements to the wording of your contracts in future. The point here is to try to put the best possible light on the situation for the customer without putting your own organization in a false light. If the customer persists in their complaint despite the fact that it is clearly unjustified, you will have to stand firm and adopt the 'broken record' technique of simply stating your viewpoint in a pleasant but firm manner until the customer gives up. But do try to be inventive and find something to offer the customer as a token of your organization's appreciation of their business.

Confirm any agreement

- Thank the customer for their help in sorting the matter out. Shake hands on the agreement if appropriate (not every customer wants to shake hands, but those who do will find this contact reassuring).
- Follow through on your promises and keep to any deadlines you agreed. Don't risk antagonizing the customer further by slipping deadlines or skimping on your commitments.

The hardest part of this plan of action is putting it into practice under the stress of the moment. It can be very hard to keep control when someone is 'blowing their stack' at you. With luck you will encounter too few really angry customers to become accustomed to dealing with them. However, angry customers may be infrequent but, handled badly, they can become nasty, so you and your staff need to practise your responses. This is why role play is such a vital part of training to handle these sorts of situations.

Devising practical role play scenarios

Ask your staff to write a brief description of the worst 'angry customer' experience they have encountered (either in your organization or elsewhere) and then use these stories as the basis of some role play exercises in which members of staff take turns to play the part of angry customers — and the rest of you practise dealing with the situation. As a manager, it is important that you participate in these exercises rather than observe them, as the chances are it will be you who will have to deal with any really angry customers, and you need to practise under pressure too!

Summary

Dealing with an angry customer calls for:

- **Self-control** — you need to distance yourself from your personal and emotional reactions so that you can handle the situation as a 'professional challenge' rather than a personal argument. It is important to keep your cool and remain assertive but non-aggressive.

- **Listening skills** — you need to find out what the real underlying problem is and to make the customer feel that someone is taking a real interest in their problems. Active listening can help to defuse anger.

- **Confidence** — you have to appear to be sure that you can handle the situation and it helps if you know what you are talking about. In-depth knowledge of your organization's policies and procedures will help you to resolve the situation in an unflustered way. If you don't know what you're talking about, the customer will lose confidence in your ability to help them and this may further provoke their rage. The bullying customer will seize on any sign of weakness or ignorance to push you into giving them what they want.

- **Action** — having talked a situation through and calmed the customer down, it is absolutely vital that you keep your side of whatever deal you have struck. You need to act on your agreements and follow through on your promises, or the customer will be back (in an even angrier mood).

To ensure that you and your staff can manage all of the above, it is essential to role play 'angry customer scenarios' as this will give you the necessary practice to deal with these usually rare situations effectively.

11
Pro-active sales action — service can mean selling too

The customer service department can have a considerable impact on increasing sales volumes. Customer care will always be a priority and long-term customer satisfaction makes a substantial contribution to the success of an organization, but this is not necessarily incompatible with seeking new business. In fact, as the customer service department is often the most regular port of call for customers and potential customers, service staff are in a prime position to identify sales leads, initiate and confirm sales.

Encouraging interdepartmental co-operation

Ideally, your department should already have an excellent working relationship with other company departments. Close interdepartmental co-operation makes it easier for the company as a whole to meet changing customer demand and provide excellent customer service. It is particularly important for the sales and customer service departments to work well together as, in many cases, their work overlaps and the input of each department can have a direct and immediate effect on the results of the other.

As a manager, you have a large part to play in initiating and developing a strong partnership with the sales department. If you feel that it's time to make some positive changes, a step in the right direction would be to arrange a meeting with the sales manager. You can use this meeting to discuss long-term mutual objectives and ideas on how to improve the way in which you work together.

Before you meet with the sales manager it is essential that you plan your approach. You must make it clear from the start that your goal is to achieve a mutually beneficial relationship and this means being prepared to give and take (see the section on negotiation towards the end of this chapter). If you start by criticizing the way the sales department operates or making demands on what you want to see happen for your own department's good then you are likely to trigger an unhelpful or defensive attitude.

You'll get better results if you try to think of some ideas that would benefit the sales department and encourage an open and constructive discussion that addresses issues which both departments could improve upon.

It would be useful to emphasize several reasons why a more co-operative relationship should be established. These could include:

- Better communication between departments decreases the likelihood of making mistakes and improves efficiency. If each department co-operates to pool customer information then it is easier to provide customers with a consistent message at all times which will help both sales and service staff to improve their performance.

- Co-operative working relationships ensure greater long-term customer satisfaction. For example, if a sales person has confirmed a particularly large order then he or she may need help from the customer service department to ensure that the customer is provided with excellent after-sales service.

- Departmental interaction provides a forum for working on ideas and developing new initiatives which benefit everyone.

- Making people feel part of a team motivates them to do well and help colleagues out.

- Successful team work leads to greater productivity.

Training staff in basic sales techniques

Although customer service may not traditionally include direct selling, encouraging service staff to actively seek new sales will benefit your company. This does not mean that staff should always aim to make a sale. For example, the customer service representative who follows sorting out a customer complaint with asking the customer to increase the order would probably lose credibility in the customer's eyes — no company should be seen to be constantly 'on the make'.

Effective customer service often means showing customers that you are there to help them 'with no strings attached', and this does not always fit in with a sales approach.

However, when it does not conflict with the customer service role, it is a good idea to ensure that your staff can spot a selling opportunity and are equipped with the basic sales skills to follow through on the opportunities that will undoubtedly arise. Remember that selling is a service too and it's your department's job to make customers aware of what your organization has to offer.

Turning customer enquiries into sales leads

When people contact your company, perhaps for further information on a product or to get a quote, it's reasonable to assume that they are considering making a purchase. So this is a clear and definite opportunity to take direct sales action.

For example, if a potential customer rings your department to get a price estimate and the customer service representative responds by supplying him or her with the price but takes no further action then there's a good chance that you'll never hear from this customer again.

On the other hand, further discussion with the customer might reveal that although your company charges more for its product, it also provides a free 24-hour help-line which the customer perceives as a valuable service. And this may clinch the sale. Informing customers about all the products and services your organization offers is central to both the customer service and the sales role.

Ensuring that your staff make the most of possible leads is the first step you need in order to establish new business. Every time a customer contacts your company, staff should be encouraged to:

- Note the name, address and telephone number of the customer.

- Find out more about the customer. Customer information is extremely valuable to your organization, so encourage staff to discover as much as they can at every opportunity. They can do this by asking questions: for example, is the customer already dealing with the company? What products are they particularly interested in? Who are their current suppliers? Do they have the full details of the products or services your company offers? Would they like to arrange an appointment? The answers to these questions should be recorded systematically so that you can build customer profiles.

You and your team could get together to think up a list of the five most important things to find out about customers on every contact. After this it may depend on how the conversation pans out as to how much more can be discovered. If the customer is in a hurry, he or she will probably be willing to supply their name, address and telephone number so that they can be sent further information or be contacted again at a more convenient time. But they may be irritated if asked too many questions. An active approach entails finding out at least enough information so that the lead can be followed up. A passive approach relies on the customer to make the decision to contact your company again and in many cases this never happens.

Once you have developed a system for establishing sales leads, you then have to decide on the next step for converting them into sales. It may be simply a matter of passing the lead on to the sales department. In this instance, it's important that you have already agreed with the sales manager that the leads will be followed up within a certain timescale. It wouldn't be fair to your staff to promise customers follow-up contacts that didn't materialize. This would make your department look inefficient, waste time and effort and waste the lead.

Taking a pro-active sales approach

If you are working on the premise that opportunities should be seized when they arise, then you may want to encourage your staff to take a more active role in confirming sales.

To do this they need to be trained to spot and exploit selling opportunities and even to initiate these opportunities wherever possible. For example, if a customer rings your company to find out about a new product launch, it's helpful if the service representative who takes the call tries to gain at least some commitment to buying while they are interested, rather than give the customer time to 'cool off' or move on to another company.

The structure of selling

Selling is a process, and like other processes, it is performed more effectively when it is done systematically. Your staff will be more effective if they are trained to structure their sales approach.

There are four clearly definable steps to selling a product or service: establishing needs, matching the product to those needs, overcoming objections and confirming the sale. It is important not to miss out any of these steps in the sales process. Each step is explained in more detail in the following.

Establishing wants and needs

The first step in making a sale is known in sales terms as the 'fact-finding' or 'probing' phase. Most products don't sell themselves and even if the customer approaches your company and seems very enthusiastic about what you have to offer, it doesn't mean that they will definitely buy your product. It is useful to find out as much about the customer as possible to assess if they are actually in the market for your company's products before launching into the 'sales pitch'.

The best way to find out more about customers is to ask lots of questions. For example:

- What do customers want, need or desire?
- How much money do they have to spend?
- When are they likely to buy?
- Which other companies have they looked at?
- What do they like about your company's product?

The aim should be to build a clear, unbiased picture of the customer's needs and, to do this, it is essential to listen carefully to the answers. There are two sorts of fact-finding questions:

1. **Open questions** which can be used to find out general information: For example, 'Where are you thinking of going on your next holiday?' 'What plans do you have to improve your productivity in the next six months?' 'Who are your main suppliers?'

2. **Closed questions** which elicit one-word answers such as 'yes' or 'no' can be used to find out more specific details and to check that the customer

agrees with what is being said. For example, 'Would you like to pay by direct debit?' 'So what you're looking for is a family car with a good safety record. Is that right?' 'Would you like to place an order?'

Matching the product to the customer

The next stage of the sales process is to tell the customer about the product, using the information that has been found out already. The fact-finding stage puts the customer service representative in a better position to understand which product will be most suitable to meet the customer's needs and also to pick the most relevant products and the most interesting features of these products to tell the customer about. In sales terms, this is known as 'feature and benefit' selling.

'Features' are the product's physical attributes: this coat is made from wool..., this microwave contains a grill..., this house is in a cul-de-sac... But it is not the features of the product that usually appeal to customers. For example, if you work in the travel business you might say that you sell holidays. If you think about it, when customers say they need a holiday, they don't actually want to 'own' a holiday. They are more likely to want the opportunity to relax, have fun or see faraway places.

In fact, nobody buys products as such, they buy the benefits that the product offers and it is important for your staff to be able get across the benefits that your product or/and company can provide. To do this successfully, it is necessary to make a distinction between the benefits and features of the product.

This means that every time a feature is mentioned it is essential that the accompanying benefit is described to the customer — as it is not always obvious. It's also a good way of emphasizing the benefit and showing how well your product suits the customer's needs. To do this it is essential that your staff have excellent product knowledge.

To change features into benefits a useful technique is to complete the description of the product with the phrase '...which means that...'. For example, 'All our engineers have mobile phones which means that you can contact them at any time throughout the day.'

Your company's products may have several benefits but they will not all be of equal interest to each customer. It's up to the customer service representative to find out which benefits are relevant to each individual — through careful questioning as mentioned above — and then prioritize these to generate the most interest.

It is also useful to drive home benefits with examples of how others have gained from using your products as people often feel more secure if they have objective proof of what your product can do for them.

You can help your staff with this by providing a list of customers with whom you have an excellent relationship and who you know to be very enthusiastic about your products. Every time your customers compliment you on the product or the service you provide ask them if you can quote what they've said to other customers. Most people will be willing to help you, but it is always a good idea to ask their permission first.

To move from the fact-finding stage of the sales process to selling the benefits it is useful to make a transition statement which should always include a compelling benefit about what you can do for the customer so that their attention is gained for what you are about to say next: 'Mr Jones, based on what you've told me about your business, it looks like we'll definitely be able to help you increase productivity!'

Review your understanding of the customer's situation by paraphrasing what they've said. This will ensure that you have understood the customer's needs. At this point, the customer can verify or correct what you have said.

Team task

It is essential that your team know what they are selling, that is, how the product can benefit the customers.

- Ask each of your staff to make a list of all the features of your product or service with a list of the corresponding benefits.

- Ask your staff to compare each other's lists and compile a full list of features and benefits.

- Ask your staff to think about your company's unique selling points (USPs). These are the benefits that only your company, your product or your service department can offer.

- Talk about how often your team tells customers about what they can gain from your product and resolve to ensure that from now on customers are told how great your company really is.

- Observe how enthusiastic your staff are about your company and what it has to offer. Remember, if staff are not excited about what's on offer, then you cannot expect customers to be enthusiastic either.

Overcoming reasons not to buy

Most customers will usually have at least some reservations about buying your product so it is important that staff are not put off when customers air their views and give reasons why they shouldn't buy. Just because a customer says, for example, that a product is too expensive, this doesn't mean that it's time to call it a day.

In sales terms, customer reservations such as, 'I don't like the colour,' 'I'm not paying that much,' and

'I'm not sure if I really need it,' are known as objections and are an inevitable part of the sales process. You should encourage your staff to take a 'problem-solving' attitude towards customer objections. The good thing about customers who give reasons for not buying your product is that they are at least considering it. This is the moment at which it is up to the customer service representative to overcome their doubts and convince them that the product is suitable for them. Viewed positively, objections can be treated as selling opportunities. When customers express reservations, encourage your staff to:

- **Empathize:** it is important to show customers that their point of view is understood. Reacting as if the customer's opinion is unreasonable or strongly disagreeing with what they say is likely to result in an argument. As seen from the previous chapters on communication, effective communication depends on a two-way flow of ideas and this is particularly important in a sales situation. Terms such as 'I can understand the point you're making...' or 'the issue you've raised is interesting...' demonstrate that the customer's point of view is valued.

- **Acknowledge:** congratulating the customer on raising their point but explaining that it's already been taken into account is a good way of reassuring the customer without actually agreeing with what they say: 'The point you make is a good one. We took this issue into account when preparing...' sounds much better than: 'That's complete nonsense, no one has ever said that before.'

- **Paraphrase:** by putting the customer's objection into their own words, staff can turn it into a question to confirm that what they've heard is correct and to find out more about the problem. For example:

Customer: 'I don't think I'll be able to afford it this month.'
Customer service representative: 'So what you're saying is that you'll be in a better position to order next month.'

* **Explain:** by providing more information it is often possible to dispel customer's misperceptions or convince them that your product is what they are looking for. For example:

Customer: 'I don't want to buy something that's going to break down after a month.'
Customer service representative: 'I can understand that. You'll be glad to know that this model has a great reputation for its reliability. Not only this but, if it did break down, we offer a free maintenance programme and a money-back guarantee if you're not satisfied. How does that sound?'

Probe for hidden objections

It's possible that the customer is harbouring a misperception about the company or is worried about something else that has not yet been mentioned — a hidden objection — so it's important to be patient and ask more questions to find out what they really mean by their objection. For example:

Customer: 'We replaced all the equipment in this company a year ago. It took my staff two months to learn how to use it and I'm not going through all that again just to speed up a few invoices.'

Customer service representative: 'I can understand that. Is your invoicing package causing you problems then?'

C: 'Well, it's a bit complicated but it's not worth buying a new system.'

CSR: 'You say a bit complicated... can you tell me in what particular areas?'

C: 'Well, actually my main problem was the time that it took to set up the system.' (Hidden objection.)

CSR: 'How long did it take?'

C: 'Well, they said two weeks and it took six! I can't face going through all that again.'

CSR: 'So if I could guarantee that the system would be up and running within two weeks and it would save you money, you'd consider changing suppliers?'

Types of objection

There are four common categories of objections that your staff should be familiar with as they come up time and again so it is important to be prepared with some ready-made answers:

Product or service

When customers say that they are not sure or don't like the product or service this often means that they don't understand how the product matches their needs. For example,

Customer: 'How do I know that it will work as well as you say it will?'

To handle this objection it's necessary to find out more about the customer's concerns and provide the required information to change their perception and build enthusiasm for the product. Testimonials from satisfied customers are useful to offer reassurance in this instance.

CSR: 'I see, so what you're saying is you're not sure that the money and time you'll save by typesetting your own reports and manuals will be worth the expense. Is that right?'
C: 'Well, I suppose so.'
CSR: 'Your concern is exactly the same as the one I heard from Colin Hudson over at Wonder Manufacturing. He originally thought that his company was too small to use DTP but he found that it paid for itself within just five months. Now your company is bigger so you'll get a quicker pay-back. How does that sound?'

Postponement

Here the customer feels no sense of urgency to make the decision so staff need to show why a decision is in his or her best interest or find out what is stopping them from making a decision now.

CSR: 'From what you've told me, we've agreed that you need and can afford this service and my goal is to help you get it. What is it exactly that's stopping you?' or 'Did you know that prices are going up next week. You'd save 10 per cent if you purchased now.'

Personal

When the customer has a personal bias it is usually based on emotion rather that fact and logic so it's important to find out more about why they feel the way they do. Perhaps they have had a bad experience with your company in the past, and need to be convinced that it won't happen again.

Customer: 'You've made it sound good but I've heard that this model breaks down a lot.'
CSR: 'I see, I am surprised as I've never heard that before. Did you get this from one of our customers?'
Customer: 'Actually it was from a friend who decided not to buy.'
CSR: 'Okay, so really everything about the package looks good to you and the main thing we have to address is the question of durability and reliability. Is that right?'
Customer: 'You could say that.'
CSR: 'Well an independent survey by *What's New?* found that this model had the best record against breakdowns and this test was against four other top brands. This means that the unit is likely to outlast any other brand. Does this reassure you?'
Customer: 'Well, I still don't want to be lumbered with a big repair bill.'
CSR: 'No problem, we have a service guarantee for the first year which means that any repairs will be absolutely free. We give this guarantee because we're convinced of the reliability of this machine and it's never let us down yet. Would you like to go ahead with the order?'

Price
Price is one of the most common objections to buying but it is often used to hide other objections so it's important to find out more about what the customer means. A good way to do this is to say: 'I understand. Could you tell me what you are comparing the price to?'

However, it's also true that the customer is often already 'sold' on the product otherwise they wouldn't be concerned about price, so making the sale may include building value in the customer's eyes.

CSR: 'I see, so if price weren't an issue we'd be in business?'

Customer: 'Well put it this way, you'd have a better chance.'

CSR: 'Do you value the reassurance of knowing you won't have to worry if repairs are needed?'

Customer: 'Yes, I suppose I do.'

CSR: 'Okay. You're right. Service Co's price is slightly less but we offer extras like free delivery which you wouldn't get there. We also offer a longer service contract which alone would more than make up for the difference in price if you ever needed repairs. So although it appears you're paying more initially, you're actually saving money in the long run. How does that sound?'

Customer: 'Well, pretty good actually.'

CSR: 'Great. Can I invoice you or do you need to give me your purchase order number?'

Steps to objection handling

Make sure your staff use the following steps when dealing with objections:

- Cushion the statement — don't become argumentative. Empathize, clarify and provide further information.

- Isolate the real objection — people often give decoy objections so ask probing questions to uncover the real objection: 'What is your main concern?'

- Give benefits — prove that the product matches the customer's needs.

- Close — gain the prospect's agreement and ask a closing question.

Confirming the sale

Even if customers seem very interested in your product, one of the golden rules of 'closing' the sale is to *ask for the order.* In some cases customers will give

what is termed a 'buying signal' which indicates that
they are interested and which, if the customer service
representative picks up on, can be converted into a
sale. For example, the customer might say: 'I'd want it
to be delivered by the end of the week...' To which the
customer service representatives could reply, 'I could
arrange that, shall we go ahead with the order?'

It is often necessary to ask for the order several
times throughout the conversation and the type of
close used can be varied to match the situation. In
some cases, a direct approach such as 'Do you want to
go ahead with the order?' may frighten the customer
off so a more subtle angle needs to be taken in some
circumstances.

Negotiation

Negotiation is an excellent skill to teach your staff
because it not only relates to making deals but is also
needed for many everyday work activities such as
raising a budget for a new project or getting new
ideas accepted. If you think about it, negotiation takes
place whenever you want something from someone
or when they want something from you.

It will be up to you to decide how much power
your staff have to negotiate and this decision will be
affected by company policy. You will also need to
make sure that your staff understand why negotiation
takes place. It's not just a matter of the customer
demanding what they want and the customer service
representative 'rolling over' in the face of
unreasonable demands. But it would be worth
negotiating if, perhaps, a customer wanted to buy
your product at a 20 per cent discount but repeat the
order over several months. The onus is on creating a

win/win situation for the company and the customer so that both parties end up with a good deal.

If you want to make the most of sales opportunities, all staff should have some authority to negotiate but you must pre-set the limits of any negotiation so that staff know what they can and can't be flexible about. It's also essential to ensure that your staff are skilled in the art of negotiation.

Preparing to negotiate

Your staff need to be able to recognize that they are in a negotiating situation and to be able to distinguish between negotiating and selling. The most important rule is that negotiation should take place *after* the selling process. This means that the customer is committed to buying if suitable terms can be agreed. The commonest mistake of negotiation is to start offering price cuts in response to objections because this doesn't overcome the objection and your company may lose profit margins unnecessarily. As discussed above, price objections are often not really about price. If the customer still has other reservations, dropping the price is unlikely to persuade them to buy. This action just devalues the product.

Staff need to decide what they want out of the negotiation and what 'concessions' they are prepared to trade for it. For example, 'If I can arrange free delivery, can you confirm the order today?'

Setting goals

It is important to define the goals of the negotiation, including what would be the best result, what could be settled for and at what point to 'walk away from the negotiation'.

Of course, staff may have no warning of many of the negotiations that they enter into and this is why it is so important that you set the limits beforehand and that your staff are familiar with them so that everyone has a good idea of what they can and cannot bargain with.

Preparing price guidelines

If possible, it is better to use any other concessions that you have to offer *before* you start trading down on price. If price is the issue and a sale can be made through a price change it is important to decide in advance how far price can be dropped while still maintaining a reasonable profit margin for your organization:

- **Top line** is the price that should be achieved if all goes according to plan.

- **Middle line** is the price that could be accepted in exchange for concessions from the other party.

- **Bottom line** is the price that would be acceptable in exchange for considerable concessions from the other side and is the lowest that can be taken under current circumstances. If circumstances change, for example, a much bigger order than originally anticipated is offered, the bottom line can be re-assessed.

Knowing what customers want

Many concessions will be tempting to the buyer but some may be of no value to him or her. The fact-finding stage of the sale should have provided this information — if not, the customer service representative needs to find out more about what the customer really values.

Trading concessions

Negotiation is about discovering what each party has to offer and exchanging 'concessions' of a similar value. It's important not to concede anything without getting something in return. Conditional offers can be used at this point. For example, 'If I could arrange free maintenance, could you guarantee placing all your business with us for the next year?'

Agreeing on terms

It is important to summarize all that has been agreed so that each person has a clear understanding of the deal. In other words the customer service representative confirms the details (and also agrees what the consequences will be if either side breaches the agreement). If the deal is complex or expensive, then it should be written down in a follow-up letter so that there can be no grounds for misunderstandings.

Summary

- Selling is a part of the service ethos and business is lost when customer service staff fail to capitalize on selling opportunities.

- Co-operation between the customer service and the sales departments is crucial. To prevent antagonism, it is important to develop shared objectives. Overlaps between departments can trigger aggravation, so hard work is often needed to build interdepartmental relationships.

- Observing a basic sales structure will make it much easier for your staff to control the direction of the sale:

  ✔ **Probe** — find out wants and needs by asking open questions

  ✔ **Match** — using the information discovered to pick out benefits of the product that match the customer's wants and needs and describe them to him or her.

  ✔ **Confirm** — gain the customer's agreement that the product does meet their criteria

  ✔ **Close** — ask for the order.

- Objections are an inevitable part of the sales process and should be viewed as opportunities to sell rather than reasons to give up.

- Negotiation is an important skill that can be used in everyday work activities as well as in sales situations.

12
Promoting customer care throughout the organization

The customer service team cannot stand alone in its efforts to satisfy your company's customers. For truly excellent service to be achieved, customer satisfaction has to be the overriding objective for the whole organization. For the customer service manager, this suggests three fundamental needs:

- The need to champion the needs/expectations of the customer to the rest of the organization — to be the 'mouthpiece' of the customer in internal discussions and decisions.

- The need to boost interdepartmental communications so that your organization operates like a consistent, seamless whole when viewed from the outside (by the customer).

- The need to ensure that the 'service chain' runs throughout the whole organization.

Championing the customer care ethos

As a customer service manager it is vital that you initiate and encourage a positive attitude towards customer care. When it comes down to it, everyone's job security depends on customer satisfaction and it is essential that all employees are made aware of this fact. Uncommitted employees from other departments can undermine the work of the customer service department as well as putting customers' backs up.

A good way to promote the customer service department's activities and to make sure that they are 'aligned' with those of the rest of the company is to start networking with other managers to find out their views and ideas and to make suggestions of your own. The aim of networking is to place yourself in as many situations as possible where you can talk about the business and the advantages that a positive attitude towards customers has on its overall success. You might want to draw up a chart of your organization and try to develop at least one contact in each department. Another good idea is to invite members of other departments to work for a day or a week in the customer service department or to invite people in for lunch to discuss the department's activities, needs and problems. Also, make sure that the customers' viewpoint is always represented at internal meetings.

Internal communication

Try to work with other departments to create a holistic organization driven by the desire to satisfy the customer. It's important to get the message across that co-operation between departments and sharing information is beneficial for the organization as a whole as well its customers.

For example, if a customer service representative has agreed to an extension of payment terms for a particular customer but fails to inform the accounts department, then payment may be demanded immediately, causing unnecessary aggravation to the customer and giving the impression that the 'right hand doesn't know what the left hand is doing'.

Any special arrangements negotiated by service staff with customers need to be clearly communicated to all other relevant departments.

Group task

To encourage interdepartmental communication and to generate new ideas for improvement arrange a brain-storming session. By working together towards an overall objective you can both boost interdeparmental co-operation and increase the understanding o f the significance of customer service throughout the whole organization.

- Ask a representative from each company department to attend the session.

- Ask the group to come up with as many ideas as they can for communication improvement. Set a time limit for this part of the session, but no other limits — people should be free to think up wild ideas if they like, as one of the purposes of a brainstorming session is to access people's creativity.

- Write down all the ideas on a flip chart or board. Don't dismiss any ideas instantly.

- Talk through each idea to see if it is viable and cross it off the list if it isn't.

- Prioritize the remaining ideas in order of importance and urgency. Perhaps pick the top two ideas to work on immediately and keep a note of the rest for a later date.

- Discuss the next step that needs to be taken to get the idea off the ground.

- Allocate responsibility for the project and agree on a deadline.

Setting goals

It may be helpful to develop a company mission statement outlining the standards of customers service that are expected.

The mission statement is a declaration of your company's goals, ideas and practices. The thought behind this is simple: if your company considers and states its goals, it's more likely to meet them. Drafting your mission statement can point staff in a positive and rewarding direction. There are several elements to consider when crafting your statement:

- Write your mission statement down as putting ideas on paper gives them value, makes them accessible and provides a ready reference. If you need more that 50 words, it's likely that your team has not focused on the essentials.

- You need to be able to live up to your mission statement so build on past performance. If your company has excelled in a particular area in the past, use the experience to improve standards even further.

- The statement should be challenging enough to stretch people to attain the stated goal. It's not designed to be a justification for sticking to the *status quo* — it's about working better and more efficiently. As goals are achieved or customer needs change, you may need to update and change your statement.

- It's important to gain your staff's acceptance as, if they don't agree with an element of the statement, they are less likely to follow the mission. Remember the mission should bring company departments together.

- Promoting your mission throughout your company — perhaps by distributing posters so that everyone has a visual reminder helps to focus employees' minds on the common goals.

Summary

Getting everyone involved in championing your customers can be a major challenge. However, it will be easier to achieve if you establish clear goals for people to focus on. Try hard to get senior management involved, as a good attitude towards customers must permeate from the top for the greatest success. Some companies require all managers to make regular service calls to ensure that they stay in touch with customer demand and opinion. Remember that your attitude will directly influence your staff's behaviour so always show enthusiasm for your department's work.

- Customer satisfaction is improved if every employee in your organization is committed to championing your customers.

- Staff will feel more motivated if they have a say in processes and systems, so get them involved in changing things for the better.

- A mission statement helps to focus your staff on the performance goal.

Index

Customer First

A Strategy for Quality Service

Denis Walker

Improving customer service is no longer a matter of choice - the future of your organization depends on it. That is the premise of Denis Walker's compelling book. Drawing on his personal experience as a manager involved in the dramatic transformation of British Airways, he sets out a model for planning, implementing and maintaining a service improvement programme designed to create competitive advantage.

The first part of the book introduces the key concepts and offers a template for auditing the service 'health' of any organization. The second part provides a framework for improvement, with examples from a range of business and public-sector activities. The third part tells the story of British Airways from 1983 to 1989 and explains how 'putting the customer first' helped to turn a slow-moving bureaucracy into a competitive and customer-responsive organization.

The book concludes by demonstrating the benefits of such a programme - for customers, for staff and managers and for all other stakeholders. According to Mr Walker salvation lies in a total commitment to customers. His book can help you and your organization to achieve it.

Gower

Dealing with Customer Complaints

Tom Williams

Increased consumer protection, government initiatives, changing expectations on the part of the consumer - a number of factors have combined to lead to a marked growth in complaints. At the same time organizations are beginning to recognize the value of an effective complaints handling system. Yet until now there has been no systematic book-length treatment of this significant area published in the UK.

Tom Williams starts by explaining the strategic importance of complaints handling. He goes on to examine how people actually complain and what their objectives might be. He shows how to determine policy and how to set up and run an effective complaints handling unit, considering both the point of view of the complainer and the implications for staff on the receiving end. With the help of case studies and examples drawn from the private and public sector he identifies the principles and practices involved. The book ends with a summary of key points and details of where to find further advice and information. This is above all a practical guide.

It is all too easy to regard complaints as a pain to be avoided or a nuisance to be got rid of as fast as possible. In fact, as Tom Williams demonstrates, they can be a valuable source of information, of customer satisfaction and, ultimately, of improvements in both reputation and profitability.

Gower

Gower Handbook of Customer Service

Edited by Peter Murley

In a world dominated by look-alike products at similar prices, superior customer service may be the only available route to competitive advantage. This Gower Handbook brings together no fewer than 32 professionals in the field, each one a recognized expert on his or her subject. Using examples and case studies from a variety of businesses, they examine the entire range of customer service activities, from policy formulation to telephone technique.

The material is presented in six parts:

- Customer Service in Context
- Measuring, Modelling, Planning
- Marketing Customer Service
- The Cultural Dimension
- The Human Ingredient
- Making the Most of Technology

For anyone concerned with customer satisfaction, whether in the private or the public sector, the Handbook is an unrivalled source of information, ideas and practical guidance.

Gower

Gower Handbook of Management Skills

Third Edition

Edited by Dorothy M Stewart

'This is the book I wish I'd had in my desk drawer when I was first a manager. When you need the information, you'll find a chapter to help; no fancy models or useless theories. This is a practical book for real managers, aimed at helping you manage more effectively in the real world of business today. You'll find enough background information, but no overwhelming detail. This is material you can trust. It is tried and tested.'

So writes Dorothy Stewart, describing in the preface the unifying theme behind the new edition of this bestselling *Handbook*. This puts at your disposal the expertise of 25 specialists, each a recognized authority in their particular field. Together, this adds up to an impressive 'one stop library' for the manager determined to make a mark.

Chapters are organised within three parts: Managing Yourself, Managing Other People, and Managing Business. Part I deals with personal skills and includes chapters on self-development and information technology. Part II covers people skills such as listening, influencing and communication. Part III looks at finance, project management, decision-making, negotiating and creativity. A total of 12 chapters are completely new, and the rest have been rigorously updated to fully reflect the rapidly changing world in which we work.

Each chapter focuses on detailed practical guidance, and ends with a checklist of key points and suggestions for further reading.

Gower

Handbook of Customer Satisfaction Measurement

Nigel Hill

With the current emphasis on service as a competitive tool, delivering customer satisfaction has become a key strategic issue. But there's only one group of people who can tell you what the level of customer satisfaction is in your business, and that's the customers themselves. Using worked examples and real-life case studies, Nigel Hill's comprehensive guide takes you step by step through the entire process, from formulating objectives at the outset to implementing any necessary action at the end.

Among the topics covered are questionnaire design, sampling, interviewing skills, data analysis and reporting, while a set of valuable appendixes points the way to sources of further information and support. The book will equip the reader both to carry out a survey themselves and to brief and monitor an external agency for optimum results.

Whether you are directly responsible for measuring customer satisfaction or simply need to understand the issues and methods involved, the *Handbook* represents an unrivalled source of knowledge and advice.

Gower

The "How To" Guide for Managers

John Payne and Shirley Payne

• Encourage your team to suggest their own objectives
• Prevent fires rather than fight them
• Decide! You'll never have all the information you would like

These, and another 107 "ideas", form the basis of John and Shirley Payne's entertaining book. Whether you're newly promoted or an old hand at managing, it will help you to improve your performance and avoid some of the pitfalls you may not even have been aware of.

Written in a practical, no-nonsense style, the Guide focuses in turn on the eleven key skills of management, including setting objectives, decision making, time management, communication, motivating, delegating and running effective meetings. A questionnaire at the beginning enables you to identify those chapters that will give you the maximum benefit. Or read through the whole book - as the authors say, using their ideas can't guarantee success, but it will increase your chances.

Gower

Interactive Marketing

Cor Molenaar

Information technology is starting to revolutionize the way goods and services are offered to, and ordered by, the customer. That is the premise of Cor Molenaar's groundbreaking book. The author, a senior member of Ogilvy & Mather's Amsterdam staff, has made a special study of the application of IT to marketing and his book was a bestseller in its original Dutch edition. With the aid of practical examples and case studies it explains why customer dialogue is the key to business success and how technology can provide the means. The possibilities include not simply access to unprecedented marketing opportunities but, for example, the chance to specify new products to satisfy customers' needs – and even ways of involving the customer directly in the production process.

The implications are far-reaching, and marketing practitioners relying on yesterday's wisdom will find life increasingly difficult. Those who survive will be those who recognize and exploit the potential of the interactive approach. A close study of this remarkable book would be a useful beginning.

Gower

The Management Skills Book

Conor Hannaway and Gabriel Hunt

There is virtually no limit to the skills a manager is expected to use. Some are required every day, others once a month or even once a year. From managing employee performance to chairing meetings, from interviewing staff to making retirement presentations, the list seems endless. How can managers be effective in all these areas? How can they know what to do in every situation?

The Management Skills Book is designed to help all managers facing the challenge of constant change. It is an easy-to-access practical reference work setting out in more than 100 brief guides the elements of the skills needed to succeed as a manager. Each guide is presented in a clear point-by-point style enabling the reader to absorb the key ideas without having to work through a tangle of theory.

New and experienced managers alike will welcome the book as a powerful aid to increased effectiveness.

Gower

Train and Develop Your Staff

A Do-it-Yourself Guide for Managers

Alan George

One of the key responsibilities of today's manager is to develop the skills of his or her people. In a small organization this often has to be done without specialist HRD staff to help and advise. And increasingly in large organizations too, the responsibility is transferring to the line manager.

In this wide-ranging guide, written for managers in this situation, Alan George looks in turn at a range of training methods, from traditional courses to work-based learning. He explains step-by-step the process of planning and providing the necessary learning opportunities. He explains, for example:

- how to determine training needs
- how to choose a suitable training event
- how to use open learning to best effect
- how to help your people to learn in the workplace
- how to assess learning outcomes
- how to develop a learning organization.

The book is designed to give all people managers the confidence to be people developers by equipping them with accessible training principles.

Gower